FULL STEAM AHEAD

FULL STEAM AHEAD

The Race to Build
A Transcontinental Railroad

by Rhoda Blumberg

NATIONAL GEOGRAPHIC SOCIETY

Washington, D.C.

I am grateful to my talented editor, Barbara Lalicki for her guidance.
I am also indebted to James P. Ronda, H. G. Barnard Professor of
Western American History, University of Tulsa, and to John White,
senior historian emeritus, Smithsonian Institution, for their assistance.
My thanks as well to National Geographic Society art director
Suez Kehl, picture editor Greta Arnold, map editor Carl Mehler,
and indexer Anne Marie Houppert.

Title page: Reproduced from a Currier & Ives lithograph
called "American Railroad Scene: Snowbound,"
which shows how rails were cleared in the 1860s.

Published by the
National Geographic Society

Gilbert M. Grosvenor, President and Chairman of the Board
Michela A. English, Senior Vice President
William R. Gray, Vice President and Director of the Book Division

1145 17th St., NW, Washington, D.C. 20036

Library of Congress Cataloguing in Publication Data

Blumberg, Rhoda
    Full steam ahead : the race to build a transcontinental railroad /
by Rhoda Blumberg. —1st ed.
        p.   cm.
    Includes bibliographical references
    ISBN 0-7922-2715-8
    1. Union Pacific Railroad Company—History—Juvenile literature.
2. Central Pacific Railroad Company—History—Juvenile literature.
3. Railroads—United States—History—Juvenile literature.
[1. Union Pacific Railroad Company—History. 2. Central Pacific
Railroad Company—History. 3. Railroads—History.] I. Title.
HE2791.U55B58 1996
365' .0973—dc20   94-34979
                                                  CIP   AC

For my husband,
GERALD BLUMBERG
whose enthusiasm for my work
goes beyond the call of duty

Contents

BRITISH NORTH

BRITISH COLUMBIA

WASHINGTON TERRITORY

OREGON

IDAHO TERRITORY

MONTANA TERRITORY

Missouri

DAKOTA TERRITORY

RUPERT'S

Fort Phil Kearny
(abandoned 1868) ■

WYOMING TERRITORY

N. Platte

Fort Laramie

Black Hills

Cheyenne

Sidney

NEBRASKA

Missouri

Columbus

Council Bluffs

Promontory Summit

Humboldt River

Reno

Truckee

Cisco

Alta

Colfax

Newcastle

Roseville

Sacramento

Sacramento

San Francisco

San Joaquin

Wadsworth

Virginia City

Truckee River

Ogden

Bear River City

Promontory Point

Great Salt Lake

Devil's Gate

Salt Lake City

Piedmont

Benton

Laramie

Julesburg

Plum Creek

North Platte

Omaha

NEVADA

UTAH TERRITORY

Green

Denver

COLORADO TERRITORY

Colorado

Site of Sand Creek Massacre

Fort Wise
(abandoned 1867) ■

KANSAS

Arkansas

Sierra Nevada

CALIFORNIA

Los Angeles

Colorado

ARIZONA TERRITORY

NEW MEXICO TERRITORY

Rio Grande

G R E A T   P L A I N S

UNORGANIZED TERRITORY

Claimed by Texas

Red

PACIFIC

OCEAN

MEXICO

TEXAS

Rio Grande

Brazos

Introduction

A rough ride—traveling in a
crowded stagecoach

IN 1832, WHEN FEW AMERICANS had been to the West Coast and even fewer had seen a locomotive, Dr. Hartwell Carver of Rochester, New York, urged Congress to build a transcontinental railroad between New York and San Francisco. Lawmakers laughed at him. They were amused again in 1838 when Mr. John Plumbe of Iowa sent a petition to Washington proposing a transcontinental railroad. One congressman declared that the idea was as silly as asking the government "to build a railroad to the moon."[1]

The dream of expanding trade and transportation from the Atlantic to the Pacific excited public enthusiasm in 1845 after a newspaperman wrote that America had a Manifest Destiny: It was the obvious (manifest) right, and God-given mission of the United States to occupy the entire continent.

Manifest Destiny was one argument adopted by Asa Whitney to promote his own grand railway project. Business with Asia was another. As a prosperous New York merchant who traded with China, he was frustrated because months of sailing were needed to transport goods from East Coast harbors to Oriental ports. Whitney argued that trains could speed goods from eastern factories and farms to western harbors where products could be shipped to China. Tea, spices, and silks could, in turn, be brought back from the Orient and sent East by train. He concluded that only a cross-country railroad could develop the wilderness west of the Great Lakes and also establish the United States as the world's principal, most profitable trader in Asia's markets.

Panning for gold

In 1848 Asa Whitney made this proposal to Congress: He would build a railroad to the West at his own expense in exchange for a land grant 60 miles wide that stretched from Lake Michigan to the Pacific Ocean. By selling off plots of this land, he was sure he could raise enough money to cover construction costs—which he estimated to be 65 million dollars, an exorbitant amount of money at that time.

Southerners wanted no part of Whitney's transcontinental line because it ran through northern states. Texas senator Sam Houston called for a cross-country railroad that would pass through his state. Senator John C. Calhoun of South Carolina declared that a transcontinental railway should start at Memphis, Tennessee. Senator Thomas Hart Benton of Missouri also opposed Whitney. He was gung ho for a transcontinental railroad—provided St. Louis, Missouri, became its main station.

In January 1848 gold was discovered near present-day Sacramento, California. In 1849 "gold fever" spread across the United States. The legendary American Gold Rush caused an incredible migration that continued during the 1850s. Thousands of fortune hunters spent months traveling to California. Some hiked, rode horseback, or used wagon trains to make their way through endless plains, over treacherous mountains, and across scorching deserts. Others chose to go by ship. Those who could afford the price of expensive tickets booked passage on steamships. Gold seekers with limited funds went in any old tub that floated. They had a tough time tolerating filth, foul food, rationed drinking water, and rough seas. Voyages on the best sailing ships usually took from six to nine months. Some old boats eventually docked in California; others were stranded along distant shores or sank at sea.

A fast track to the goldfields seemed crucial, not only for individual gold seekers but also for the government. Trains racing cross-country could quickly transport California's wealth to Washington. Also, soldiers and supplies could be speedily shipped to western military posts that had been established to stock provisions for travelers and protect the country from "wild Indians."

However, northern and southern congressmen were so bitterly opposed to each other that the railroad issue was at a standstill. In 1853, hoping to break this gridlock, Congress asked the secretary of war, Jefferson Davis, to dispatch five survey teams to investigate both northern and southern routes between the Mississippi River and the Pacific coast. When the surveyors handed in their reports, it was not surprising to learn that Davis, as a staunch Southerner, chose a Deep South route through Texas. He even persuaded President Franklin Pierce to buy Mexican land as part of a rail line's right-of-way.[2]

Northerners opposed Jefferson Davis's route because it would enable the South to gain economic and political power in the undeveloped West. Plans for a transcontinental rail line were deadlocked, and prospects for its construction seemed slim.

In addition to dissenting congressmen, there were people who objected to their country being overrun by "mechanical demons" that spit fire, exhaled filthy smoke, spewed burning cinders, and screeched ear-splitting noises. Railroads not only disturbed the peace and beauty of the landscape but also caused calamities. Stoves that heated wooden coaches were known to tip over and set cars on fire. Badly graded roadbeds caused derailments, and engines occasionally exploded.

Riverboat, stagecoach, and freight wagon companies were hostile because trains competed with them. Merchants, manufacturers, tavern keepers, and tradespeople were also troubled. They didn't want any transportation route to bypass the stores, taverns, and factories they had built along existing roads.

These people opposed the first railroad bridge that spanned the Mississippi River. This great link between the East and the West was completed by the Rock Island Railroad in 1856. It connected Rock Island, Illinois, with Davenport, Iowa.

Two weeks after the Rock Island Bridge was opened for traffic, a boat named *Effie Afton* slammed into one of the bridge's piers, burst into flames, and burned part of the bridge. The boat's owners sued the bridge builders, claiming that the bridge was a menace to navigation. They argued that any structure spanning the Mississippi River was dangerous for river traffic.

Many people in Rock Island and Davenport were sure that

the *Effie Afton*'s collision was not an accident but rather a deliberate act of sabotage plotted by riverboat operators and businessmen who wanted to control commerce along the Mississippi River.

An able attorney represented the bridge owners. Declaring that "people have as much right to travel east and west [by rail] as well as north and south [by river]," this lawyer convinced the courts to favor the railroad company.[3] The decision received nationwide publicity.

This pro-railroad lawyer was to become a pro-railroad president. He was Abraham Lincoln.

Riverboats on the Mississippi

FOLLOWING PAGES:
A cartoonist's fanciful version of a fast transcontinental trip

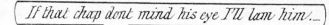

PART 1
Getting Started

1 "Crazy Judah"

Theodore Judah
"Crazy Judah"

PEOPLE CALLED HIM "CRAZY JUDAH." He was viewed as a harmless, harebrained lunatic because he didn't think that canyons and mountains were obstacles for railroad builders. Judah seemed to spend all his waking hours trying to convince anyone he met that trains could cross the Sierra Nevada Mountains. Sacramento grocer Newton Booth is said to have been the first to call him "Crazy Judah." The term was adopted by other Californians who believed that Judah's ideas sounded insane.

Unlike many visionaries, Theodore Judah was a clear-headed, well-qualified engineer. He had shown signs of genius as a child growing up in Troy, New York. When only 11 years old, he had attended advanced science classes at his hometown's Rensselaer Polytechnic Institute, and when he was 13, he was hired to be a surveyor's assistant for the Schenectady & Troy Railroad. By the time he was 25, as chief engineer in charge of building the "impossible" Niagara Gorge Railroad beneath the famous falls, he had become one of America's outstanding railroad engineers.

FACING PAGE: Surveyors for the railroad lug their instruments as they climb up steep rocks.

Sea Routes to California

Summoned to California in 1854 when he was 28 years old, he built California's first railroad during the frenzy of the Gold Rush. The Sacramento Valley Railroad officials who hired him paid more than a hundred men to grade a short roadbed from Sacramento to Folsom, which was in gold-mining territory. The railroad company had gone to the expense of having iron rails and heavy locomotives shipped from the East around Cape Horn by clipper ship. But Judah was disappointed because the rails stretched only 21 miles. He had finished this job in seven weeks and wanted to continue on, building a train route over the towering Sierra mountains, then across the desert to the Utah Territory.

However, company officials were not interested in investing further, especially because costs would mount if rails went up mountains.

Peaks 12,000 feet high didn't faze Judah. They merely heightened his desire to build a transcontinental railroad. After completing his job with the Sacramento Valley Railroad Company, he disappeared into the Sierra for weeks at a time, probing deeper and deeper until he was sure he had discovered a route through the range.[1] Although the going would be rough for tunnel diggers and blasting crews, Judah was confident that iron rails could be imbedded through the mountains, then eastward across the continent.

Theodore Judah made four trips to Washington between 1856 and 1859, to convince congressmen that a railroad could and should stretch across the land. He talked about adding anti-slavery states to the nation and argued that train lines would become iron bonds that would tie California's allegiance to the North. This was of great concern because Northerners worried that Southerners in gold-rich California might favor secession.

In 1859 Judah set up a "Pacific Railroad Museum" in the Capitol, with an impressive display of landscape paintings and maps, along with geological specimens that he had collected in the Sierra. However, he could not budge congressmen. States were threatening to secede from the Union. This was the overwhelming issue—not trains on plains and mountains.

Disheartened but not discouraged, Judah distributed a pamphlet which he had written and published at his own expense. It was called "A Practical Plan for Building the Pacific Railroad."[2] He sent copies to President Buchanan and to every member of Congress, informing them that in addition to California "there is Utah, Oregon, Washington, the Russian possessions, the Sandwich Islands [Hawaii], China, and the Far East Indies—all of which are brought more or less within the influence of this road." "Its profitableness," he wrote, "will exceed that of any known road in the world."[3]

Frustrated because his ideas had not been adopted, Judah returned to California in 1860 to gather more concrete facts that would justify building his railroad. He surveyed and mapped a railroad route over the Sierra. Then he drafted a document to form a Central Pacific Railroad Company. However, he could not convince congressmen to back him. He had to seek private support.

The Big Four

Friends at Dutch Flat and neighboring California mining camps invested $40,000—a small but encouraging beginning. Judah needed $110,000 more to make his Central Pacific Railroad a legally recognized corporation entitled to sell stock. He was sure San Francisco's free-spending millionaires would back him. Yet no one was interested. Why risk money on a railroad when investing in gold mines yielded solid profit? Judah also faced outright hostility from many businesses. The Sitka Ice Company, for example, didn't want California mountains to be the source of ice when their specialty was importing it from Alaska. Stagecoach, wagon-

Collis Huntington

Leland Stanford

train, and riverboat companies were opposed to competition from railroads. They denounced Judah's scheme as unsound.

Discouraged, Judah traveled to Sacramento to continue canvassing for funds. In November, 1860, he invited local businessmen to hear him speak at the St. Charles Hotel. "Your property, your business is here; help me," he said. "...You will have control of business interests that will make your fortune in trade."[4] Judah informed his audience that he had crossed the crest of the Sierra at least 23 times, and was confident that trains could travel through these mountains safely. Afterward, there were some handshakes,

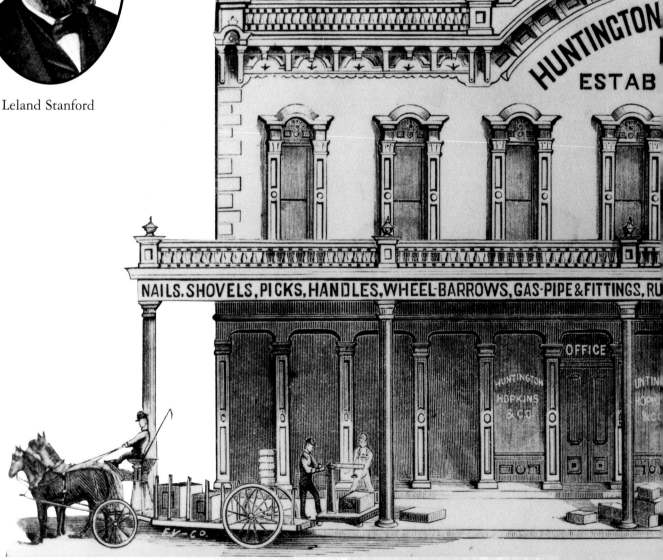

many admirers, but no backers. However, one merchant named Collis Huntington asked Judah to drop by his office to provide details.

A meeting was held in Sacramento above the largest, most prosperous hardware store in the West. It was owned by Collis Huntington and his partner, Mark Hopkins. These men were intensely interested, and so were two of their pals: Charles Crocker, who owned a dry goods store, and Leland Stanford, who operated a wholesale grocery business. Each of these four men had left the Northeast to seek their fortunes during California's Gold Rush. Gold mining by others made

Charles Crocker

Mark Hopkins

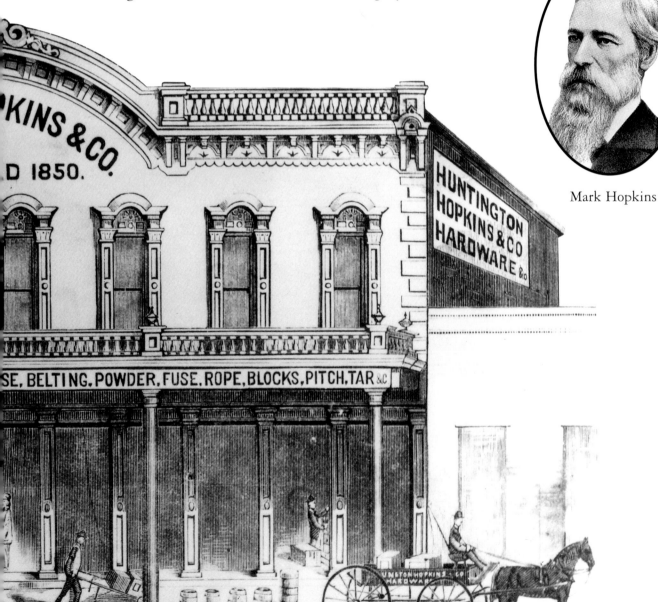

them rich; they sold supplies to miners and settlers.

At the time this meeting took place Lincoln had just been elected president, and Stanford was campaigning to run for governor of California as a candidate of the anti-slavery Republican Party.

The four shopkeepers were fascinated by Judah's ideas, not because a transcontinental railroad would be a grand national enterprise, but because of the money-making possibilities. Hordes of people hoping to strike it rich had been stampeding into Nevada after silver was discovered there in 1859. They needed food, clothing, and mining equipment. These supplies were being dispatched from San Francisco and Sacramento by wagon and muleback over rocky, winding

At the very time fierce Civil War battles were taking place, Northerners were planning a transcontinental railroad.

Sierra mountain roads. The deliveries were snail-paced, and rates were exorbitant.

Theodore Judah sold these businessmen on the prospect of speeding their goods to Nevada's rich silver mines. The thought of shipping trainloads of products to new towns beyond the Sierras was irresistible. It didn't take genius to see that quick rail service would kill the competition.

Lincoln's election had triggered the secession of 11 southern states. On April 12, 1861, the Civil War started when Confederate guns fired on Fort Sumter in Charleston Harbor. Southern congressmen quit Washington to return home and help the Confederate cause. As a result, there was no one in Congress to oppose a transcontinental railroad that

would run through northern states. President Lincoln called its construction "a political as well as military necessity."[5]

Like most Californians, the shopkeepers were pro-Union. Realizing that the time was ripe for backing from Washington, they organized the Central Pacific Railroad Company on April 30, only 18 days after war had been declared. Leland Stanford was president; Collis Huntington, vice president; Mark Hopkins, treasurer; and Charles Crocker, construction supervisor. Because they controlled the new railroad, these men became known as the Big Four.

As chief engineer, Theodore Judah was sent to Washington in October 1861 to request money and land from the government. Carrying one thousand prints of his surveys, Judah gave copies to President Abraham Lincoln and to every senator and representative in Congress.

He was a brilliant spokesman. Calling the transcontinental railway a war measure, he argued that by shipping gold and silver from California and Nevada, iron rails could carry wealth to the North. He stressed the need to keep California and the West linked to the Union. He also emphasized that a new railroad could transport troops rapidly to army posts and trouble spots west of the Mississippi.[6]

A New Law

Judah had no problem persuading congressmen to endorse his ideas. President Lincoln was particularly elated when he signed The Pacific Railroad Act of 1862 into law because he had made a campaign promise to endorse a transcontinental railroad. He had repeatedly declared that "a railroad to the Pacific Ocean is imperatively demanded in the interests of the whole country.... The Federal Government ought to render immediate and efficient aid in its construction."[7]

The Act of 1862 specified that the Central Pacific

Railroad Company would start at Sacramento, California, and lay tracks to the California-Nevada boundary. Also, a new corporation called the Union Pacific Railroad Company was to be formed. It could be operated by any individuals who bought stock and put up money to help build the line. Union Pacific rails were to start at the Mississippi River and continue west until they joined those of the Central Pacific—*at a location that was not specified.* If the Union Pacific reached the California border before the Central Pacific did, it could continue building; if the Central Pacific arrived at the border first, it could proceed to build eastward, and join the Union Pacific *anywhere.* When both companies joined tracks and linked up with railroad lines east of the Mississippi, they would create the country's first transcontinental railroad.

The government would pay each company in government bonds: $16,000 for each mile of track in the flatlands; $32,000 for more difficult terrain; $48,000 for mountains. Handling mail and transporting military men would bring additional profits. There would be no "Indian problem," because the Pacific Railroad Act stated that the government "shall extinguish as rapidly as may be the Indian titles to all lands falling under the operation of this act."[8]

The Pacific Railroad Act awarded the Central Pacific and Union Pacific rights-of-way extending 200 feet on either side of the tracks, and alternate sections of public lands on either side of the line—6,400 acres for each mile of track. This property was to be given only after each forty-mile section of rails was completed. But once given, the company could sell or lease the land to settlers.

Although the act offered extremely generous terms to lure investors, it contained a worrisome clause that stipulated "all iron used in the construction and equipment of said road to be American manufacture."[9] The railroad companies were forbidden to buy British iron, which was readily available at one-third the price! Thaddeus Stevens, a congressman from

A glorified view of
the ground-breaking
ceremony,
January 8, 1863

Pennsylvania, had demanded insertion of this clause. In addition to his official duties, he was an iron manufacturer, and he represented the largest iron-making state in the Union.

A government-sponsored transcontinental railroad became a real project because of "Crazy Judah." Before he left Washington, both the Senate and House issued a joint testimonial thanking him for his "valuable assistance in aiding the passage of the Pacific Railroad Bill through Congress...." The testimonial stated that Judah's "explorations and surveys in the Sierra Nevada Mountains...enabled many members to vote confidently on the great measure."[10]

Californians received the news by telegraph. They were so jubilant they celebrated with fireworks, torchlight proces-

sions, and grand parades. A reporter for the Sacramento *Union* wrote that a mile-long fireman's parade was "the most brilliant affair of its kind that has ever taken place in this city."[11] Signs held high read, "The Pacific Railroad—Uncle Sam's Waistband"; "Married...Mr. Atlantic to Miss Pacific"; "Little Indian Boy, Step Out of the Way for the Big Engine."[12]

The Big Four resolved that "commencement of the work on the railroad of this company be inaugurated with proper ceremonies."[13] Scheduled for January 8, 1863, this groundbreaking ceremony took place after a flood on a muddy street in Sacramento. A local newspaper noted that "the choice of scene for the ceremony was not favorable to the presence of the gentler sex.... The great preponderance of pantaloons was a disagreeable necessity of the 'situation.'"[14] Stanford shoveled dirt into puddles. Crocker called for nine cheers in place of the usual three, and a crowd knee-deep in mud complied with wild enthusiasm.

After this hoopla, Judah became increasingly upset that his ideas were being ignored by Crocker, Hopkins, Stanford, and Huntington. The Big Four were uncomfortable because their brilliant engineer wasn't like them. Making money was not his main concern. They excluded him from their business meetings, knowing that Judah would be shocked by their slick dealings.

They were right. Judah was horrified by their tactics. Stanford, who had been elected governor of California in 1861 for a two-year term, used his authority to earmark more than a million dollars of the state's money for his Central Pacific Railroad. Then Huntington hired some geologists who were willing to swear that the mountains started 7 miles from Sacramento. In reality the Sierra foothills started 22 miles from the city!

Nevertheless, distracted by war, United States officials accepted the geologists' conclusions without investigation. Huntington was elated. He had moved mountains! Instead of $16,000 per mile for flat land, the Central Pacific would receive $48,000 per mile for tracks laid on relatively level ground. As a result, the company would obtain an additional $480,000 from the federal government.

Judah was appalled. The Big Four plotted another sleazy scheme: the creation of the Crocker Contracting Company, their own construction business. The cronies hired themselves to work for the Central Pacific, then overcharged the company. They awarded contracts to themselves—and they paid themselves 90 million dollars for labor and materials that cost only 32.2 million dollars.

They had created their own "gravy train."[15]

Judah was so upset that he headed for New York City

hoping to find investors who would buy out the Big Four. Rather than board a ship that rounded Cape Horn to reach the East Coast (and which could take months) he chose the most rapid route: He set sail for Panama, traveled by train from the Pacific to the Atlantic side of the isthmus, then boarded a ship to New York. Judah arrived in New York 23 days after he had left California, on October 26, 1863, the very day the first Central Pacific rails were set. Thirty-seven-year-old Judah never saw those rails. He died from yellow fever, contracted while crossing Panama.

2 Stalled Near Mountains

NOW THE BIG FOUR DIDN'T HAVE a qualified engineer to guide rail setters through the towering Sierra Nevada. But that didn't faze Charlie Crocker. Even though he wasn't a trained engineer, he took charge. This go-getter had made a living since he was ten years old working as a newsboy in Troy, New York. After that he had plowed fields and worked as a woodcutter, blacksmith, teamster, and miner, before becoming a merchant. Charlie Crocker was an energetic 250-pound dynamo who knew how to push his weight around. He could roar orders and keep things moving. He boasted, "I know how to handle men."[1] Building a railroad was far more exciting than measuring out yards of cloth for customers in his dry goods store.

Collis Huntington was another partner who knew little about building railroads, yet proved to be useful because of his business acumen. Son of a poor Connecticut tinker, he supported himself at the age of 14 by working on a neighbor's farm for seven dollars a month and board. He left this job one year later. After that he peddled jewelry in Ohio and Indiana,

Central Pacific Railroad workers

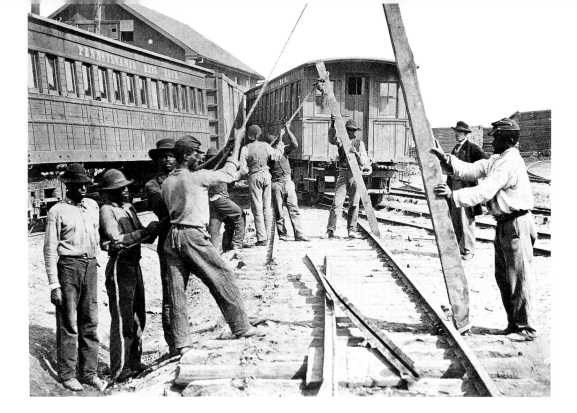

Back East, former slaves were taught how to rip up rails as part of the Union's Civil War effort.

worked as a bill collector in the South, sold butter in New York City, and established a country store in Oneonta, New York. At the start of the Gold Rush in 1849, Huntington headed for California, not to realize a miner's dream, but to try his luck as a merchant selling miners' supplies. His shrewdness at bargaining made him an ideal purchasing agent for any business.

Obtaining supplies was Huntington's responsibility. Explosives required for construction were sold in the East where war was raging. Iron products, such as locomotives, rails, spikes, and nails were also manufactured in northern factories in the East. These products were needed by the Union Army. Competing with military orders made prices sky-high. Huntington became a welcome customer because in addition to dollars—and sometimes instead of money—he gave away gifts of Central Pacific stock.

This brilliant businessman also talked investors into lending money to the Central Pacific. As a result he was able to ship six locomotives, a number of passenger cars, boxcars, and at least 25 flatcars 14,000 miles from New York around Cape Horn to California. Northerners' ships were lucky not to be stopped by Rebel warships whose captains were eager to plunder their cargoes of powder and iron. Some of the vessels reached San Francisco within four months, but one of them, delayed by storms that drove it back from Cape Horn twice, arrived from the East after a harrowing six-month voyage.

By the end of February 1864, more than a year after the ground-breaking ceremony, only 18 miles of track had been laid. The Central Pacific line now stretched from Sacramento to Roseville. To publicize their railroad, the Big Four staged a grand celebration. Hundreds of guests attended a railway excursion. Members of the California state legislature and their families were seated in bright yellow cars furnished with gorgeous imported carpets. Less important guests sat in the open air, on hard benches atop seven flatcars. A ten-man brass band performed atop another flatcar.

When the train reached the end of the track, everyone got off and enjoyed a picnic of food and wine that "brought gladness to everyone's hearts."[2]

Guests were impressed and enthusiastic about the Central Pacific Railroad. Crocker and his cronies were elated, even though they knew that this small stretch of railroad was just the beginning of a huge construction project.

The next objective was Newcastle, 13 miles from Roseville. But short of equipment, short of men, and short of cash for the project, it took one year to complete this segment. Then work came to a standstill. The company was not eligible for government aid until its workers had completed 40 miles of track. Since construction costs were more than the Big Four had estimated, they were reluctant to invest more of their own money. At one time there wasn't a nickel in the company treasury. No tunnels had been built, and there would have been no light at the end of them had they been constructed. State aid came to the rescue in January 1865 as a result of Governor Stanford's political clout. In exchange for

Mrs. Strobridge (second from the left) entertained visitors at her home-on-wheels.

funding, the Central Pacific Railroad agreed to transport the following, free of charge: granite for public buildings, state troops, animals, "lunatics, and paupers."[3]

When the Civil War ended in April 1865, demands for rails by the army diminished, and factories were delighted to keep Huntington as a customer. However, the railroad

company was short of laborers. Because digging for gold still lured men to mining fields, it was hard to find workers in California. Crocker did manage to recruit 2,000 men in 1864. When the railroad reached Colfax, California, in September 1865, 1,900 quit. Some used their earnings to buy stagecoach fare from Colfax to Nevada's gold and silver mine districts. Others quit rather than move forward and face dangerous work on steep mountains.

To help him recruit and manage men, Crocker had hired a construction boss, James Strobridge. "Stro" was a burly Irishman from Vermont. He had started working as a track-layer on railroads when he was 16, and later became a contractor who built railroad lines in Connecticut. He had gone West during the 1849 Gold Rush and had done some mining, farming, and freighting before working as a construction foreman on the San Francisco & San Jose Railroad. Loud-mouthed and quick-tempered, he controlled his workers by shouting and cursing—and settled arguments with his fists.

Strobridge set up headquarters in a passenger car which he transformed into a home-on-wheels. His wife and six children moved in. Mrs. Strobridge was the only woman who moved with the line. She added a delicate touch to rough life in the wild. By adorning her "front porch" with an awning, hanging plants, and a cage with a canary at the entrance, she symbolized domestic bliss for lonesome, homesick laborers. A newspaperman praised her as "the heroine of the Central Pacific" and declared that her home-on-wheels was so neat and gracious it "would not discredit San Francisco."[4] However, evenings with the wife and kids didn't alter Stro's mean temper. Furious outbursts occurred especially because he was short of manpower. After each payday men quit to head for the mines in Nevada.

Strobridge and Crocker stormed about in a futile search for more workers. Then Crocker hit upon an idea: Why not hire the Chinese?

James "Stro" Strobridge

Vicious bigots attacked Chinese immigrants.

3 "Not a Chinaman's Chance"

IN 1850 THERE WERE ONLY a few hundred Chinese in California. Most of them were merchants whom others respected as honest, upright citizens. Californians called them "celestials" because they had come from the Orient's "Celestial Kingdom." By 1852, as a result of the Gold Rush, there were at least 20,000 Chinese on the West Coast. Their skill as miners caused jealousy and hatred. Accused of taking American gold away from land that belonged to United States citizens, "John Chinaman" was attacked by hoodlums on San Francisco streets, reviled by columnists in California newspapers, and chased by miners from diggings in the goldfields.

Even though Leland Stanford employed Chinese houseboys, he found it politically wise to call the Chinese a "degraded" race of undesirable immigrants who were unfit for honest labor. The California Legislature had passed a law in 1858 forbidding the importation of Chinese, but this did not stop immigration from China. The demand for Chinese houseboys and farmers' helpers was so great that the law was not enforced. Chinese crossed the Pacific in increasing numbers because ships' captains made enormous profits when they overcrowded their vessels with them. Most passengers were poor peasants from the southern coastal regions of China.

Strobridge hated the thought of hiring "Orientals." Believing they were "heathen weaklings" qualified at best for washing clothes and raising vegetables, he barked at Crocker, "I will not boss Chinese....They're not fit laborers."[1]

But the Chinese immigrants were eager for work, and at least 5,000 men were needed for the grim job of blasting roadbeds around and through mountains. At that time the Central Pacific construction crew numbered less than 800, and many of these workers were threatening to strike for more pay. By the spring of 1865, the situation had become so critical that Crocker convinced Strobridge to hire 50 Chinese on a trial basis. The construction boss was willing to overcome his prejudice because he so desperately needed to get on with the job.

Herded into freight cars at Sacramento and hauled to the end of the track, "celestials" were immediately put to work. Annoyed crews shouted insults at "coolies" (a derogatory term for unskilled Asiatic workers). They calmed down only after they learned that the "Orientals" would not mingle with them. The Chinese, also, felt more comfortable—and safer—camping and working segregated from the others.

At first Strobridge gave the Chinese unskilled jobs, such as filling dump carts, because he believed they were too weak to swing heavy hammers. However, the labor shortage made him test their muscle power, and after a few days he ordered them to try grading a roadbed. What a surprise! Stro was told, "The coolies' right of way was longer and smoother than any white crew's."[2] According to one observer, this was "the cruelest blow of all to the ego of the whites." Some of them got so angry, they quit.[3]

Strobridge asked Crocker to find more "coolies." Within

Thousands of Chinese who were hired to work on the railroad crowded ships sailing from China to California.

six months 2,000 more Chinese were hired. Since not enough workers could be found in California, Crocker made arrangements to have shiploads of men brought from China.

The Chinese Protective Society, which had been organized by San Francisco clergymen, met ships with armed guards to protect immigrants from being physically attacked by vicious bigots.

Brokers in Hong Kong, Canton, and Macao recruited most of the newcomers. They usually advanced passage money and got their money back (plus interest) from wages the Chinese earned while working in the United States. Like indentured servants, these immigrants could not return to

Tea carrier

their homeland until they had paid all debts. However, many brokers guaranteed to ship bodies back to China free of charge if workers died in California.

Chinese workers were paid between $25 and $40 a month. They were organized into groups of from 12 to 20 men. Each group had its own cook and a headman who knew a smattering of English. A white boss was usually the overseer. Once a month Charlie Crocker rode his horse along the construction route. He cheered workers on, dumped money from two saddlebags into headmen's hats, then trotted away. The headmen distributed wages—but only after deducting money for food, provisions, and maintaining campsites.

Irish immigrants made up most of the remaining workforce. They earned more than the "celestials"—at least $40 a month, and the company paid for their food and housing. The Chinese, dubbed "Crocker's pets," were not only better workers and less costly, but also less troublesome. Instead of getting drunk, fighting, and disrupting nighttime quiet—like some of the other railroad workers—they were polite, withdrawn, and orderly. After a 12-hour workday, the Chinese enjoyed hot baths, using heated water that cooks carried to them in discarded whiskey barrels and empty gunpowder kegs. Each man soaped, rinsed, and dabbed himself with sweet-smelling "flower water" before putting on clean clothes and sitting down for his evening meal.

Cleanliness of this kind was truly foreign to quite a few railroad laborers who didn't bother bathing. They voiced one of the popular insults of the day: The Chinese were like women, "smelling of perfume."[4]

These "Oriental heathens" were also accused of eating "un-Christian foods." Instead of meat, beans, and potatoes, they ate seaweed, dried fish, strange vegetables, and rice. Rumor had it they cooked cats, rats, and dogs, too. During the day, white workers relieved their thirst with water, not caring whether it was slimy or muddy. They didn't know that impure water could make them sick. John Chinaman drank tea in tiny cups "ladies see fit to use."[5] Several times each day hot brewed tea was brought to them by their cooks. It was carried in powder kegs suspended from the ends of bamboo poles. Tea made with water that had been boiled was purified. And so, because they drank tea, the Chinese workers avoided the stomach ailments that afflicted others.

By June 1865 "coolies" were working so efficiently that Strobridge was able to establish a construction camp 92 miles from Sacramento at Cisco, in the Sierra. For the next three years this was to be the supply depot for tunnel and mountain construction. Stro was a general commanding an army of men. His biggest, best troops were the "celestial Chinese." Crocker pointed out that these men were descendants of people who built the Great Wall of China. In fact, for thousands of years these remarkable people had been constructing shrines, temples, and palaces perched on mountain peaks. To them, precarious locations were poetic, and overcoming the difficulty of construction was a tribute to Heaven and to China's Divine Emperor.

Chinese workers risking
their lives at Cape Horn

Before reaching the high peaks of the Sierra Nevada, Stro
reached an impasse, a stone wall, a nearly perpendicular cliff
that rose 4,000 feet above the American River. Americans
nicknamed this gigantic spur of granite in the Sierra "Cape
Horn" after the fearsome cape at the tip of South America. It
loomed as a dead end that could bring work to a standstill.

A Chinese interpreter told Strobridge that his people would be able to tackle the towering cliff efficiently. However, they needed to weave waist-high baskets that were each big enough to hold at least one man. Bewildered, but willing to listen, Stro sent to San Francisco for straw.

The Chinese wove round baskets of the kind that had been used as cliff-hangers in their homeland for 2,000 years. Eyelets on four sides needed for ropes were painted with good luck symbols. Men were lowered in baskets from the summit to work on the cliffside. Each basket had a two-man hauling crew at the top of the cliff. After being lowered, workers used chisels and blasting powder to attack Cape Horn. Dangling a thousand feet up in midair and swaying in the wind, each man chipped and drilled into rock, inserted explosive charges, and lit fuses. The nimble workers had to signal their hauling crews to pull them up quickly before the charges erupted. Explosions killed many, yet the work went on because there were always immigrants from China to replace casualties.

The work on Cape Horn had started during the summer of 1865. By May 1866 the Chinese had carved a narrow ledge on it. Then, standing on this ledge, they created a roadbed wide enough for train tracks.

Thousands of Chinese workers had conquered Cape Horn. Strobridge was so impressed he declared that Chinese workers were "the best in the world. They learn quickly, do not fight, have no strikes that amount to anything, and are very cleanly in their habits."[6] Stanford was another who had changed his opinion of the Chinese whom he had once called "the dregs of Asia."[7] In a government report he praised them as "quiet, peaceable, patient, industrious and economical—ready and apt to learn all the different kinds of work required in railroad building." He was also delighted to note that when compared to white laborers they were "contented with less wages."[8]

During the summer of 1866, the Big Four gave a party to celebrate the Central Pacific's progress—and to attract addi-

FOLLOWING PAGES:
The largest curved trestle of its time, near Secret Town

Rounding Cape Horn

tional investors. Ten carloads of guests left Sacramento and traveled 74 miles by rail, to Alta, California, where they enjoyed an elegant picnic that included the finest foods and a choice of the following beverages: lemonade for the ladies, ice water for the anti-alcohol males, and "Pacific Railroad Punch" with liquor for the rest.

Digging In

After Cape Horn, the highest peaks of the Sierra still separated the railroad workers from Nevada. At least 15 tunnels were needed to penetrate these mountains. The longest, 1,659 feet, would have to pierce through a peak called the Summit, which was more than 7,000 feet high.

This had to be accomplished at a time when there were no trucks, tractors or giant earthmovers.

Crocker sent 500 Chinese accompanied by engineers to start this Summit Tunnel during the spring of 1866 at the same time that others were completing their work on Cape Horn. The Chinese drilled, hacked, and blasted at rock, then shoveled and carted the debris away. The granite was so hard that picks and chisels were constantly replaced because they quickly became blunt. Work progressed at a rate of seven to twelve inches a day! Pecking away so slowly was maddening, but the Chinese were tenacious and the work went on.

When Governor Stanford learned about these tedious procedures, he suggested a new device, a steam-powered drill that could speed digging. Several of these were sent to Stro, who stubbornly refused to have his men use newfangled tools. However, to speed things up, he did adopt the use of nitroglycerin, a dangerous explosive that was used in Europe. Because it was risky to transport safely, Crocker hired a Scottish chemist to mix the formula near the workmen. Accidents took place as a result of nitroglycerin explosions in tunnels. For example, when Stro went inside the Summit, a delayed blast shot slivers of rock into his face and destroyed one of his eyes. Whenever the deadly substance was not handled with extreme caution, Chinese workmen were killed. The toll in lives was dreadful.

In his rush to get the work done more speedily, Crocker hired Cornish miners who had been working in Nevada's gold and silver fields. They were famous for their skills as underground laborers. He put them to work at one end of a tunnel. He put some Chinese to work at the other end and was amazed to find that "the Chinese, without fail, always out-measured the Cornishmen."[9] After that Crocker was content to leave the tunneling to his "celestials."

The winter of 1866-67 was one of the worst on record. There were 44 snowstorms that varied in length from short squalls to a two-week gale. Whipping winds created snowdrifts 40 feet high. Roadbeds were buried. Gangs of workers shoveled in vain because they couldn't dig into the huge mounds of hardened snow. Tracklaying stopped. Work in the open was impossible. However, tunnel construction continued.

The Chinese burrowed down like moles. When their

A backbreaking job—
clearing roadbeds

shacks were buried under snow, they built chimneys that pierced the snow, and poked air shafts to the outside for ventilation. They also excavated passageways from their living quarters to their workplaces. These cold, dark, subterranean trails enabled them to work both day and night. Building the Summit Tunnel took 13 months. It was the last major tunnel in the United States to be gouged by hand.

The second winter, 1867-68, also proved to be harsh. The Big Four decided they could not afford to stop construction because of the weather. Obtaining provisions and other supplies was a major problem that had to be solved. Their company shops at Sacramento designed, built, and sent on a gigantic snowplow to clear rails. It was so huge that 12 wood-burning locomotives had to push it. But even this 30-foot-long, 10-foot-high monster machine was often stopped in its tracks by hard-packed snowdrifts.

Small sleds were pulled by Asian manpower because horses could not survive the extreme cold and the icy footing. Hundreds of Chinese hitched themselves to enormous log sleds whose runners had been greased with fat for better traction. Battling blizzards, they hauled three locomotives and 40 cars for 15 miles. To do this, they first had to cut a path 200 feet wide through the forests on mountainsides. They felled giant redwood trees, many of them well over a hundred feet high. Then, to have smooth roadbeds, they uprooted the stumps with explosives, which caused chunks of rocks, roots, and wood to shoot out, often killing workers.

Thousands of Chinese used pickaxes to expose frozen roadbeds. Snowslides were killers. Entire camps of Chinese were buried, and the bodies of the men were not found until the spring thaw.

People used "not a Chinaman's chance" as a catchphrase to describe the horrible plight of those who worked on the railroad. No one kept count of the appalling number of casualties. Men fell off cliffs, froze to death, were buried alive, and were blown up by explosions. One newspaper reported that as a result of their dangerous jobs, ten tons of Chinese bones—the remains of 1,200 Chinese—had been shipped back to China from the Sierra for burial.[10]

Hard-packed snow could stop this monster machine.

4 Tracks Across the Desert

TUNNELS, ROADBEDS, AND RAILS had been completed across the mountains by the end of 1867. Strobridge had followed orders from Sacramento headquarters that he was to "rush construction as fast as men and money would do it."[1] Nevertheless, it took three years to breach the Sierra.

As a result of their free spending, the Big Four faced big problems. Once again the Central Pacific's treasury was practically bare. Bookkeeper Mark Hopkins was terribly upset by the extravagance and enthusiasm of his partners. He couldn't understand how Stanford and Huntington were able to wheel and deal their way through life by borrowing money and purchasing products on credit. Hopkins couldn't dampen their optimism. However, he managed to convince Huntington to sell the hardware store they both owned so that it would bring in some much-needed cash.

Crocker tried to help the money crunch by cashing in on the Sierra Nevada Mountains' frozen assets. He created the Summit Ice Company, just as the Sitka Ice Company had feared. Ice was cut into blocks and sent from mountain ponds

FACING PAGE:
The Central Pacific built sheds to protect tracks from snow.

and streams to populated places in California. Unfortunately, not enough money trickled in, and in 1870, after three years, the business had to be dissolved.

Crocker had also started an irrigation business at the end of 1867. He channeled streams, built aqueducts, and constructed reservoirs to catch water from springtime thaws in the Sierra. This subsequently proved profitable for the Big Four, and for California's farmers. However, during 1868 and 1869 the enterprise didn't make enough to matter.

The Central Pacific faced financial ruin. The company had been trapped in the mountains, unable to get its trains on a fast track. How frustrating, because the government had promised the Central Pacific generous aid for each mile of construction! Once past the Sierra, the Big Four determined to race across flat land. Only then would their iron horses win big cash prizes from Washington.

The Sacramento *Union* newspaper discouraged public enthusiasm, calling the Central Pacific a "poor, starving, frozen thing which the credulous public warmed into life by its charities."[2] It insisted the Central Pacific would never become part of a transcontinental railway; that snows would keep the line closed at least five months of the year.

The newspaper did concede that the Central Pacific Railroad wouldn't be a total loss, because its trains could be used by holiday travelers who wanted to spend cool summer vacations in the scenic Sierra.

To proceed, to send rails and provisions to building sites, railroad tracks in the High Sierra had to be kept open. Shoveling was futile, because winter snows continuously blanketed the ground. During the summers of 1867 and 1868 Crocker hired hundreds of carpenters to put roofs over rails in locations that suffered the heaviest snowfalls. Thirty-eight miles of snowsheds protected trains from the furies of future winters.

After laying rails down the east slope of the mountains, construction workers crossed the Nevada border. On May 1,

Snowdrifts could be higher than telegraph poles.

The roundhouse at Truckee, after a snowstorm

1868, they halted at a small settlement on the Truckee River called Lake's Crossing. Some wag described the place as having a "population of two men, one woman, three pigs and one cow."[3] However, this unimpressive cluster of shacks had a strategic location. Less than 20 miles from Nevada's silver mining center, Virginia City, Lake's Crossing was an important supply stop for miners. Crocker negotiated with Mr. Lake, who owned the settlement, and bought most of his property for the Central Pacific so that train yards, company shops,

and a railroad station could be built as quickly as possible.[4]

A land agent hired by the Central Pacific held a public auction of town lots, which sold at anywhere from $600 to $1,200 each. Within days buyers erected 200 stores and shacks. When Crocker realized how quickly the place was expanding, he put up his own money and bought 40 choice acres for himself. He named the new town Reno, in honor of a Union officer, Gen. Jesse Lee Reno. Within a year Reno, Nevada, had a population of more than 15,000 people. It became a rowdy town with a sizable number of saloons and gambling houses.

On June 17, 1868, the first passenger train traveled 154 miles from Sacramento to Reno. The locomotive, *Antelope*, pulled a car crammed with thrilled passengers around sharp curves and up steep mountain slopes until it was 7,000 feet high in the sky, surrounded by snow. Nervous but exhilarated travelers were relieved when their train descended "swiftly and smoothly down the mountains into the great basin of Nevada." A reporter for San Francisco's *Alta California,* who was aboard for this inaugural trip, declared that he had traveled "the greatest highway yet created for the march of commerce and civilization around the globe."[5]

"The greatest highway" soon extended past Reno. As construction gangs raced ahead, they entered land occupied by Shoshone and Paiute Indians. Strobridge was glad to note that they were not troublesome, "one reason being that General P. E. Connor was sent out with a thousand soldiers a few years before [1863] and he cleaned up the country, destroying men, women and children indiscriminately."[6] To guarantee peaceful relationships with the survivors, Crocker called a "powwow." After introducing himself as a "big chief" who had thousands of warriors under his command, he offered them a "treaty." It allowed tribal chiefs to ride passenger cars, and their people to ride freight trains, free of charge. The agreement was signed and sealed with an ornate railroad stamp.

Although some of the other travelers were delighted to gawk at "savages" who had passes to ride the trains, some complained about them. They did not want to occupy cars with people who looked dirty and "pestered passengers for money and eatables."[7] Chiefs were soon demoted from coaches to baggage cars, or they were allowed to hang on to the outside of trains. That way, no one was offended—except the poor Native American.

Stro hired both male and female Indians to work alongside the Chinese. One observer was amazed to watch women

The Central Pacific paid Paiute chief Winnemucca to become a tourist attraction.

handling crowbars and sledgehammers so well that "they out-did the men."[8]

According to one of the Central Pacific's engineers, some Paiutes teased the Chinese by telling tall tales about monster snakes in the area that were so huge they could swallow a man whole.[9] Although they had not been terrified by the dangers of cliff-hanging in the Sierra, hundreds of Chinese became so frightened that they took their belongings and fled, heading for the West Coast. It was no laughing matter for Stro. He sent men on horseback to round them up, reassure them, and lead them back to work.

Thirty-five miles past Reno, Crocker staked out the town of Wadsworth as another railroad terminal. Then Stro and his Chinese army marched into the broiling Humboldt Desert. Many overland emigrants bound for California had died in this wasteland.[10]

Temperatures rose to 120 degrees. Special flatcars fitted with huge tanks had to be brought in so that the workers could have water. Strobridge was upset because "there was not a tree for 500 miles of the route that would make a board."[11] Lumber for tracks and firewood had to be hauled hundreds of miles from Sierra forests. The only redeeming feature of desert work was that the land was flat and dry. Therefore, there was no need to construct tunnels and bridges. Central Pacific workers raced over the desert so quickly that during one record-breaking day they laid six miles and 800 feet of track.

Moving forward at full speed made the Central Pacific eligible for additional government aid. After reaching Wadsworth, which was 189 miles from Sacramento, the United States Treasury enriched the company by handing over more than ten million dollars. Additional money was promised if the Department of the Interior approved the quality of construction.

In September 1868 government railroad commissioners

arrived to examine the tracks. If construction passed their scrutiny, the Central Pacific would collect $30,000. Charlie Crocker accompanied them on their trip from Sacramento to Reno, and a newsman was aboard to record events for the *San Francisco Chronicle.* In his notes he reported that Crocker made sure everyone was in a festive mood. "Whenever the engine stopped to get water," he wrote, "any of the party could take a drink [of liquor].... In truth we became hilarious...and all went as merry as a marriage bell." The commissioners inspected the rails in the following manner: One of them stood on the platform of the rear car, used a small spyglass, and peered at the ties and rails. Another lay down on the floor of a train, shut his eyes, and took a nap. "The argument being this, that if the passengers could sleep the track must be level, easy, and all right; whereas, if too rough to sleep, something must be wrong with the work." Fortunately for the Central Pacific, "the commissioner slept profoundly"—sure proof that he was either drunk, weary, asleep on the job, or that the ride was smooth and as soothing as a lullaby.[12] Government aid was given as a result of this trip to slumberland. Now the Big Four could sleep well, too!

Stro kept his battalions on the move as though he were advancing against an enemy. The Big Four truly felt threatened by another army: Construction troops of the Union Pacific Railroad Company, who were advancing from the east. Both companies wanted to cover as much territory as possible, because they were being paid by the mile. According to the Pacific Railroad Act these contestants for American dollars were to meet head-on and link rails. The Big Four hoped to sprint ahead so that the eventual meeting place would be as far east as possible. It would mean more territory and more money for them. Officials of the Union Pacific were formidable opponents pushing towards the West Coast, intent upon stretching their track as fast and as far as they could. Both companies were engaged in a race with no set finish line.

FOLLOWING PAGES:
The Union Pacific
crossed Indian land.

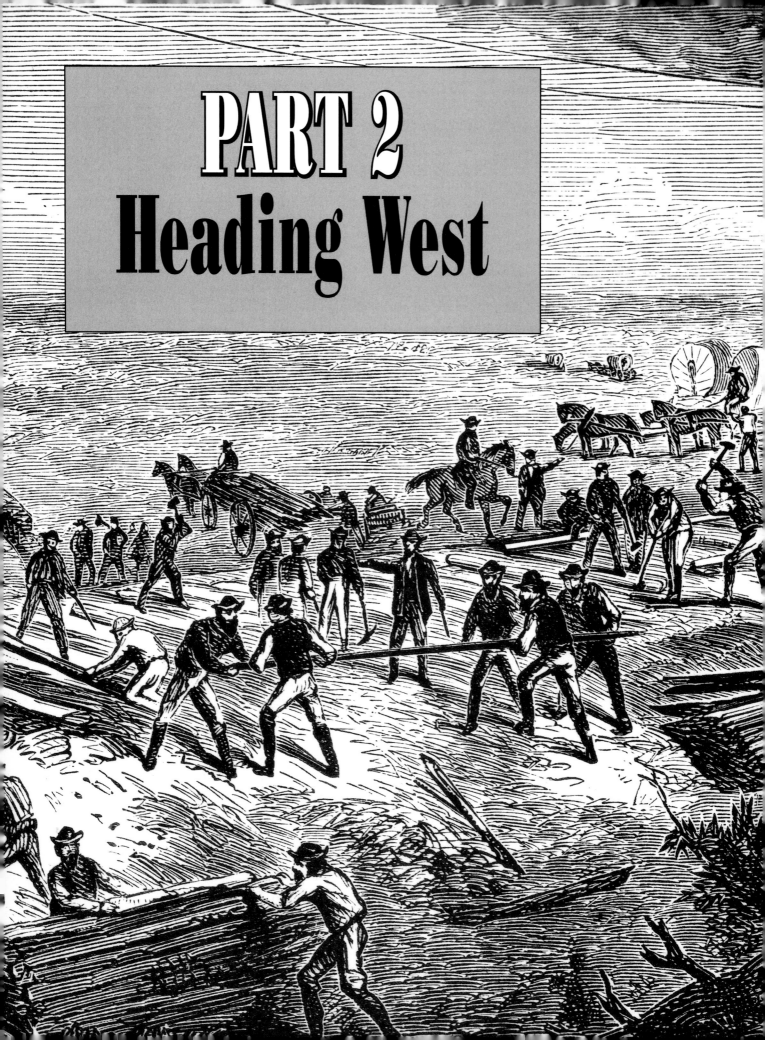

PART 2
Heading West

Thomas Durant

5 The Rival Railroad

THE RIVAL UNION PACIFIC RAILROAD COMPANY
was led by Thomas Durant of New York City. Although he
had graduated with honors from Albany Medical College and
enjoyed being called "Doctor," his obsession was making
money. Instead of practicing medicine, he played the stock
market and became a director in the New York City branch
of his family's successful export business. Known as an extravagant party-giver who strutted about in loud-colored suits
and lush fur-trimmed coats, Durant's ambition was to make
millions at full speed. He believed he could ride a fast track
to great riches if he gained control of the Union Pacific.

According to the federal government's Pacific Railroad
Act of 1862, two million dollars in stock had to be sold before
construction of the Union Pacific could begin, but no one
person was allowed to own more than two hundred thousand
dollars worth of stock. Realizing that this restriction hobbled
his power, Durant used his talents as a great persuader. During
1863 he induced friends and acquaintances to buy stocks by
lending them money to do so. After they purchased shares in

their own names, he bought the stocks from them! It was a slick trick that sidestepped the law.

The cunning doctor had complete control of the company. During a stockholders' meeting, he chose Maj. Gen. John Dix to be president of the Union Pacific. As a former senator and secretary of the treasury, Dix had important political connections. From Durant's point of view, he was an ideal choice for another reason. Dix was too occupied with his Civil War duties as commander of the Union Army's Department of the East to pay attention to business. Durant was content to be "vice president and general manager" because he was really in complete charge of the Union Pacific.

The government had not specified the exact place where constructing the Union Pacific was to start. Through friends in high places Durant managed to visit President Lincoln at the White House to discuss the matter. As a result, an executive order designated the starting point as "the western boundary of the State of Iowa...within which the City of Omaha is situated."[1] Did this mean that the track should begin at Council Bluffs, Iowa, or at Omaha, Nebraska? The government's statement may have been deliberately vague because it was politically wise not to create animosities by designating the exact location.[2] Residents at Council Bluffs interpreted the president's order to mean that construction would start in their town. However, Council Bluffs was located on the east bank of the Missouri River. Durant was not going to waste time and money building a bridge. Therefore, he chose to begin grading at Omaha, which was on the west bank.

Durant staged a ground-breaking ceremony in Omaha on December 2, 1863. Crowds cheered as soldiers fired salutes and a succession of speakers extolled the occasion. Durant's close friend, George Francis Train, an eccentric who dressed flamboyantly and made exaggerated pronouncements, was master of ceremonies. "The Pacific Railroad is the nation," he shouted, "and the nation is the Pacific Railroad.... This is

FULL STEAM AHEAD

the grandest enterprise under God."[3] The audience roared approval, and Mr. Train was very pleased—especially because he had bought a sizable amount of land in Omaha. He planned to sell and enjoy big profits as soon as Omaha became an important railroad junction.

Train was passionate about building iron rails across America. He envisioned "a chain of great towns across the continent, connecting Boston with San Francisco by a magnificent highway of cities."[4]

He talked about making Columbus, Nebraska, the new capital of the United States because it was located near the center of the country—and because he owned hundreds of acres there.

However, the Union Pacific didn't have enough money to start construction. During the winter of 1863-64 Durant went to Washington, armed with cash and stock certificates to bribe congressmen. Collis Huntington was at the Capitol, too, his pockets crammed with money that he gave to politicians for the good of the Central Pacific. Both men convinced corruptible lawmakers that the transcontinental railway must have additional government aid. Handing out payoffs may not have been necessary because most congressmen were ardently pro-railroad. However, both Durant and Huntington hoped that their bribes would ensure quick passage of laws that would benefit their companies.

A new Pacific Railroad Act was passed and signed by President Lincoln on July 2, 1864. The act increased the amount of government money both railroad companies could obtain. It eased terms for private investors and

George Francis Train

doubled the size of land grants—from 6,400 to 12,800 acres per mile. Both Durant and Huntington were pleased.

Construction of the Union Pacific started in March 1864, three months after the ground-breaking ceremony. Gangs of men dug up some muddy streets in Omaha. They were helped by 15 women of the Omaha tribe who earned 50 cents a day for backbreaking labor. This was obviously not the way to jump-start a momentous enterprise. An army of workers had to be hired. However, the company's treasury was practically empty. Not a single rail was set in 1864, or during most of 1865.

Durant's friend, George Train, always had intriguing ideas. He had become a shipping magnate in Boston while still in his teens. When he was 24 he introduced canned goods, prefabricated houses, and the American-made Concord coaches to Australia. He also started the use of horse-drawn streetcars in England, wrote pamphlets, published a newspaper, and ran a brisk business exporting products from New York City; Liverpool, England; and Canton, China. This fantastic fellow was the ultimate egotist, who gleefully described himself as "that wonderful, eccentric, independent, extraordinary genius."[5] Feeling just as desperate as Durant about the Union Pacific's predicament, Train brainstormed a solution.

A Sleazy Scheme

George Train knew about a corporation in France that had profited at the expense of the government when it erected public buildings. He had little trouble convincing Durant that they must form a construction company with the same name as the one he admired in France, the Credit Mobilier. The new company with its fancy title and fraudulent aims would be awarded building contracts by the Union Pacific at enormously high rates. It could charge any price it wanted. Profits from construction were guaranteed because of government money.

Federal funds would pay the bills. It was an ingenious way to get building started and was similar to the Big Four's Crocker Contracting Company. Durant was delighted. He became president and principal stockholder of Credit Mobilier. Using his authority as vice president of the Union Pacific, he engaged the Credit Mobilier to build the first hundred miles at $50,000 per mile.

Peter Dey, the Union Pacific's honest chief engineer, knew that the actual cost was no higher than $30,000 per mile. Obviously, Durant and his henchmen intended to pocket the difference! Dey was horrified, and was doubly shocked to hear that Durant had added an unnecessary nine miles to the route out of Omaha. Silas Seymour, the assistant engineer, was a "yes man" ever ready to oblige Durant. He sketched a roadbed that formed a loop to lengthen its distance. Nine more miles meant more money from Washington, and 115,200 more acres from government land grants.

Dey was so upset that he sent in his letter of resignation. He wrote that he was giving up "the best position in his profession this country has offered to any man.... I do not care to have my name so connected with the railroad that I shall appear to endorse this contract.... I cannot willingly...swell the cost of construction."[6] Durant wasn't bothered by Dey's resignation. His main concern was making money.

George Train set off for Boston to promote Credit Mobilier. He fished for backers and hooked one of New England's wealthiest men, Oakes Ames, a congressman from Massachusetts. Oakes and his brother, Oliver, had made their fortunes as shovel manufacturers. Known as the "Kings of Spades," they were smart enough to see the money-making possibilities of a railroad construction company linked to the Union Pacific. The Ames brothers invested a million dollars in Credit Mobilier, and their friends put up an additional 1.5 million dollars.

As a result, construction moved along.

Rail station in Omaha, Nebraska, spring of 1866

In November 1865, when 17 miles of track had been laid, Durant decided to publicize this progress. He arranged an excursion for 20 celebrities, including a famous guest of honor, war hero Gen. William Tecumseh Sherman. The Civil War had ended the previous April, and Sherman was now in charge of all the troops of the Great Plains as commander of the Military Division of the West. Four years before the Civil War started, Sherman had expressed his belief that a transcontinental railroad was vital to America's future. Its construction he called "a work of giants," adding that "Uncle Sam is the only giant I know who can grapple the subject."[7] To please Sherman, his name was painted in gilt letters on Union Pacific's Locomotive Number 1. As there were no passenger

cars, guests sat on a flatcar using nail kegs as chairs. They wrapped themselves in buffalo robes to keep warm. At the end of the track the group picnicked and listened to a succession of long-winded speeches praising the Union Pacific. Sherman sounded skeptical. "This is a great enterprise," he said, "but I hardly expect to live to see it completed." Although pro-railroad, he believed construction would be held back by raiding "bold and bloody Sioux and Cheyennes."[8]

By the spring of 1866, the frontier village of Omaha, Nebraska, had been transformed into a booming railroad town. There were shops with machinery for building railroad cars, a brick roundhouse for ten locomotives, and hundreds of houses for railroad workers and their families. As a result of the war's end, swarms of men had headed west, looking for jobs. Soldiers who had been released from both the Union and Confederate Armies, some freed slaves, and many Irish immigrants joined the workforce.

Omaha became the headquarters for construction, even though its out-of-the-way location on the western frontier side of the Missouri made delivery of supplies difficult and, therefore, very expensive. The nearest railroad station was on the other side of the river, 150 miles away. Ox-drawn wagons

Wood for construction had to be shipped from faraway places to the treeless plains.

carrying freight had to be ferried across. Transporting cargo on the Missouri was a nightmare. Submerged trees and sandbars made the river treacherous, and its waters were not navigable most of the year. Winter brought ice, spring caused floods, and in summer the river was often too shallow for large boats.

Rails and machines had to be brought to the frontier from eastern factories. Because local cottonwood was soft and rotted quickly, tons of hardwood had to be hauled great distances, from Michigan, Wisconsin, and Indiana.

The cost of transporting good wood from faraway forests was too high for Durant to stomach. He decided to use cottonwood that had been "burnettized," soaked in a solution to retard rot. The processed cottonwood did get heavier, and it was used for railroad ties. It still rotted—but not immediately. Burnettized cottonwood was not a good substitute for hardwood, but long-range problems were of little importance to Durant. He was not ashamed to say that he wanted to "grab a wad from construction fees—and get out."[9] He had no grand patriotic visions about binding the nation together. A transcontinental railway was merely his private road to riches.

It was lucky that Durant hired Maj. Gen. Grenville Dodge as the new chief engineer. General Dodge was an idealist who, like Judah, dreamed about building a first-rate iron road that would connect and unite distant sections of the United States.

6 An Army on Wheels

Union Pacific workers lived in cars like these.

GENERAL DODGE DECLARED that he would not accept the post of chief engineer unless he was given "absolute control.... There must be no interference."[1] This tough talk annoyed Durant, but he needed Dodge badly.

As a former surveyor for the Mississippi and Missouri Railroad, Dodge had explored enormous expanses of land in Iowa and Nebraska. During the Civil War, he had made a name for himself as a fighter and as an expert who repaired rail lines that had been ripped up by the Confederates.

Durant had been trying to hire Dodge for years. In 1862 and 1864, after Dodge had been seriously wounded by bullets during Civil War battles, Durant expected to lure him away from the Union Army, but failed. As soon as Dodge got back on his feet, he returned to the battlefield, determined to continue fighting for Union victory. He promised to join the Union Pacific as soon as the war was over.

However, after the war Dodge remained in the U.S. Army. General Sherman had assigned him to command all military operations in Kansas, and in the Nebraska, Colorado, Utah,

Gen. Grenville Dodge

and Dakota Territories. His orders: to clear the way for the Union Pacific Railroad by "removing" all Indians. General Sherman considered the railroad a "military necessity and as the one thing positively essential to the binding together of the republic East and West." He regarded the railroad as "the solution to Indian affairs" because troops and supplies could be dispatched quickly to western army outposts where soldiers protected travelers and settlers against hostile natives.[2]

After a while Sherman realized that Dodge was the only qualified engineer who knew the Great Plains, could fight Indians, and was also an expert at railroad construction. Therefore, he gave him a leave of absence from the Army so that he could be employed by Durant.

Dodge welcomed the chance to become the Union Pacific's chief engineer. When he took charge in May 1866, only 40 miles of rails had been set, even though groundbreaking ceremonies had taken place two and a half years earlier, in December 1863. The lack of progress was maddening, especially because it was common knowledge that the Central Pacific had hired thousands of Chinese who were already digging tunnels in the Sierra Nevada. The Union Pacific needed a leader to charge ahead and order an army of workers to conquer distances quickly.

No one knew which route the railroad should take. Surveying parties had disbanded after being attacked by Indians. Within 30 days, Dodge plotted rights-of-way, and arranged to have military guards accompany surveyors.

When he had been fighting hostile Crow Indians in the Rockies during 1865, Dodge had discovered a low pass across the mountains in Wyoming's Black Hills. Realizing it was not too steep for locomotives and freight trains, he had made a note of its location. When he became chief engineer for the Union Pacific, he used this pass to plot the part of his railroad route that went through the mountains.

Some months before Dodge took charge, former

Brig. Gen. Jack Casement had been hired as construction boss. Jack and his brother, Dan, had a contract to lay all tracks for the Union Pacific. Dan was in charge of the books. Jack, in charge of the men, was a fierce-looking character, notorious for holding a bullwhip in his hand and keeping a huge-handled pistol in his belt. However, it was not the force of appearance that made him the engine that

Brig. Gen.
Jack Casement

made men work; rather, it was his genius as an organizer.

After Dodge took over and arranged for supplies of iron and wood to be delivered from Omaha, Jack Casement was able to invent an "army on wheels"—a town-on-rails that consisted of as many as 22 cars. Trains contained supplies, carpenters' and blacksmiths' shops, general stores, water tanks, kitchens, mess halls, and washhouses. There were windowless boxcars called boarding trains where workers slept in bunks that were three tiers high. Bedbugs and bad air caused many workers to rig up makeshift tents outside on the ground alongside the cars or up high on the trains' roofs.

Horse-drawn wagons carried supplies to the workers.

78

Hundreds of men lived at the end of the track in boarding trains and tents. After laying track they moved forward every few days. Horse-drawn wagons that carried provisions and supplies followed. Herds of cattle to be butchered for hearty meals moved along with them.

Each car was equipped with racks for rifles and carried piles of ammunition—to be used in case of an Indian attack. Those camping outside slept with guns at their sides. Since many of the workers were veterans of either the Union or Confederate Armies, they knew how to muster arms fast.

Guns weren't needed at the beginning, because the first

150 miles west of Omaha was Pawnee country. The Pawnee were friendly, and pathetically poor. During the 18th century at least 10,000 Pawnee had thrived on the plains. By the mid-19th century their numbers had dwindled to less than 5,000 due to cholera (carried by white emigrants) and casualties from battles against the Sioux. After most of their land had been ceded to the United States through treaties (1833, 1848, 1857), many of their braves became scouts in the Army. They were hired by Dodge as armed escorts. Issued uniforms and guns, they were posted along the railroad line under the supervision of white officers, who relied on the Pawnee to fight their traditional enemies, the Sioux.

At the peak of tracklaying, there were at least 10,000 workers. Construction was organized as efficiently as a military operation. A supply train with thousands of rails, ties, and spikes constantly shuttled between Omaha and the end of the line. Horse-drawn wagons carried these supplies to the workers. Iron men, five to a rail on each side of the track, lifted 500-pound rails and dropped them in place. Then spikers hammered spikes through rails into the ground with perfect rhythm: three strokes to a spike, ten spikes to a rail, four hundred rails to a mile. The procedure was so effective that laying at least a mile a day became the rule. And when

the Casements offered extra tobacco and double pay, crews covered as many as eight miles in one day. "General Jack" had put together efficient teams made up mostly of Irish immigrants. Dodge described them as "the best organized, best equipped and best disciplined work force I have ever seen."[3]

The track soon reached the 100th meridian of longitude, 247 miles west of Omaha. Durant decided to celebrate this event in October 1866 with an "extravaganza," a lavish, spectacular party that could become the sensation of the century.

"The Great Pacific Railroad Excursion"

Invitations were sent out to millionaires, members of Congress, and foreign diplomats, all cordially invited to bring their families. Rutherford B. Hayes, future President of the United States, and Robert Todd Lincoln, the son of the late president, one Scottish Earl, and two French noblemen were among the 200 people who were delighted to accept. Important Union Pacific officials attended, although the Ames brothers refused to come because they condemned the excursion as an extravagant waste of company money. John Dix was another no-show, because he was about to resign as president of the Union Pacific and accept a diplomatic post as minister to France. Oliver Ames would become the Union Pacific's new president.

Newspaper reporters were, of course, part of the party, and two "official photographers" were paid to document this grandest of excursions. A Mr. C. L. Jenkins was hired to set up a portable printing press so that he could publish a daily newspaper to chronicle the travelers' adventures. To be assured of superb food, one of Chicago's most famous chefs commanded the kitchen. Two "tonsorial artists" (barbers) were available to trim gentlemen's mustaches, sideburns, and whiskers. A magician was included to make sure there was never a dull moment. Durant also engaged two musical bands, one from Chicago, Illinois, and another from St. Joseph, Missouri, to keep spirits at a high pitch.

A telegram from Durant alerted Dodge that "a large number of Eastern capitalists and their families" were on their way. The general rounded up friendly Indians for Wild West atmosphere, hired guides for buffalo hunts, and made arrangements for comfortable camping on the prairies.

Most of the guests had to ride five different railroad lines in order to reach St. Joseph, Missouri. Then they boarded two deluxe riverboats that had been rented by Durant for a two-day gala voyage to Omaha. Dinner was memorable. The menu listed 30 main courses, including the following western specialties: saddle of elk, braised bear, larded antelope, roasted wild turkey, and puree of rabbit. After that, diners enjoyed an assortment of 18 pastries, a variety of other desserts, mounds of fruits, and pyramids of candies. Ladies and gentlemen who were not too stuffed to move danced away the night as musicians played under the light of an October moon.

A guided tour of Omaha proved impressive. The travelers admired the many buildings that had been erected for the Union Pacific. Guests enjoyed another extravagant banquet and ball. Silas Seymour, the Union Pacific's consulting engineer, was a participant who chronicled the adventures and reactions of excursionists for a book that was published the following year, titled *Incidents of a Trip Through the Great Platte Valley to the Rocky Mountains and Laramie Plains in the Fall of 1866.* He gloated because excursionists were "delighted, and somewhat astonished to find themselves, after a week's journey westward from New York, still among people of wealth, refinement, and enterprise."[4]

The Great Pacific Railroad Excursion officially began the next day. Two wood-burning locomotives adorned with American flags and deer antlers pulled nine cars westward.

Riverboats brought the guests to Omaha, Nebraska.

Adventuresome Easterners took their seats in four brand new passenger coaches that were furnished with heavy silk drapes and deep, plush carpets. An elaborate parlour car featuring rare woods and exquisite silk chairs was set aside for members of Congress and other important people. Durant used the famous "Lincoln car" for himself, his family, and close friends. He had purchased this ornate coach after it had brought the assassinated President's body from Washington to Illinois. There was a "refreshment saloon" where men could enjoy liquor, cigars, and "male" conversation, a "cooking car," and a car for luggage and supplies.

FOLLOWING PAGES:
Groups of Indians were paid to entertain tourists.

Travel was deliberately slow so that travelers could enjoy seeing the prairies. Seymour reported travelers' fears that "Indians might be watching us from some surrounding crags and coveting our scalps as trophies for the adornment of their wigwams." He noted, however, that most of the party felt safe, knowing that armed guards protected them. Their spirits were soothed by band music and by magnificent scenery that "elicited exclamations of wonder and admiration from all."[5]

The excursion train pulled into Columbus, Nebraska, where a huge campsite had been set up near the station. It was lighted by campfires and torches. After supper, Pawnee braves wearing only breechcloths and war paint staged a tribal dance. Their "wild and hideous yells" were frightening, especially for straitlaced ladies and proper gentlemen. One of the wives reacted in approved 19th-century female fashion by fainting when one of these near-naked Indians jumped in front of her.

Everyone had to be assured that "the Indians were entirely friendly," but guests were not told that the Pawnees had been acting. They had been paid to put on a show.

After being assigned tents, everyone bedded down on straw mattresses, cozy under buffalo robes. At three o'clock in the morning guests were "startled from their slumbers by the most unearthly whoops and yells of the Indians," who were brandishing tomahawks, screeching, and stomping on the ground in front of the camp. The Pawnees were following instructions from Dodge. The general immediately realized that he had gone to extremes in his efforts to create a Wild West atmosphere. He and Durant quickly made the rounds to assure panicking people that the noise was merely a harmless "savage morning serenade for their own particular amusement."[6]

More marvelous adventures awaited excursionists the following day. The train stopped for two hours at a Pawnee camp to watch a staged battle. Thirty Pawnee horsemen disguised as enemy Sioux warriors attacked. Blank cartridges were used as they fought, howling and shouting. After ear-splitting noises and frenzied attacks and retreats, the Pawnees "conquered" the invading Indians.

As a reward for their performance, Durant presented the Indians with trinkets, but he did not reveal to his excursionists that the show had cost him hundreds of dollars. According to Seymour, guests found it "most amusing to see these greedy savages," and they enjoyed gawking at "squaws" with papooses on their backs.[7] He also noted that all Indians were called "low and brutal...slightly, if at all, above the level of the beasts."[8] The performances that had been carefully planned by Durant and Dodge reinforced these prejudices.

The train chugged along until it reached the 100th meridian of longitude. Photographers worked nonstop while guests posed for pictures under the "100th Meridian" milepost, which had been erected for the occasion. A telegraph office had been set up so that guests could send messages home.

For the second night's camp-out Dodge made sure that no one worried about being scalped or killed by Indians. He arranged to have United States soldiers camp close by, within view of all excursionists. The next day Durant offered male guests the choice of a buffalo hunt or an antelope hunt. Professional guides had rounded up the animals in droves so that amateur hunters would have no trouble shooting them. One group of men experienced the scare of their lives when Sioux Indians confronted them and took their buffalo meat away. According to Seymour, the Indians "spared their lives only on condition that they should never be found again upon their hunting grounds."[9]

Late in the afternoon the train stopped at the end of the line. Travelers were entranced as they watched Casement's men lay 800 feet of track in 30 minutes. Another memorable

FACING PAGE: (upper)
Curious travelers visited
an Indian camp.
(lower) Thomas Durant,
leaning on the left post,
and others posed at the
100th Meridian marker.

night was planned. This time, the entertainment was refined. There was a band concert, one hour of fireworks, and a lecture on phrenology by a well-known "bumpist," Professor Wells. He chose to examine the skull of that eccentric, successful millionaire, George Train, "the humorist of the party."[10] The professor analyzed Train's personality after feeling for bumps on his head—a procedure that was unscientific, but in vogue at that time.

On the return trip to Omaha, people spent two hours touring a vast prairie dog town. They marveled at the animals who peeped out, then disappeared into the ground so fast that, despite hunters' efforts, only one was shot.

Durant was intent upon having this excursion end in a blaze of glory. The train stopped so that everyone could watch a huge prairie fire—deliberately set by workmen who were following Durant's orders!

Passengers were elated by their experiences. They would enliven parties at home with their chatter about the beauties and horrors of the "Wild West." Seymour praised the excursion as "the most important and successful celebration of the kind that has ever been attempted in the world."[11]

Knowing that sensational stories stimulated circulation, newspapers featured lurid tales about the prairies. Indians were portrayed as loathsome enemies of society. The idea of an untamed, uncivilized country filled with dangerous savages was engraved in the minds of readers.

The excursion did produce the result Durant wanted. The Union Pacific received nationwide publicity, and descriptions of its accomplishments attracted investors who purchased millions of dollars worth of Union Pacific bonds.

A peaceful picture of Sioux life

7 "Wild Indians"

BOOKS AND NEWSPAPERS KEPT EMPHASIZING that "wild Indians" held back the country's development. Native Americans were called ignorant, primitive, immoral beings who were trying to stop civilization's march of progress. Many people viewed them as a pestilence on that vast ocean of undeveloped land, the Great Plains. Samuel Bowles, a prominent Massachusetts travel writer, expressed a more charitable view than those who wanted "the indiscriminate extermination of the savages, as of wolves or other wild beasts and vermin." He described Indians as "vagrant children" who should be treated "as a father would treat an ignorant, unde-veloped child. If necessary to punish, punish." Even though he stated that the Indians were cheated when they signed treaties, Bowles wrote, "We know they are not our equals; we know that our right to the soil, as a race capable of its superior improvement is above theirs.... Let us say [to the Indian]...you are our ward, our child, victim of our destiny, ours to displace, ours also to protect." He believed that the government could "protect" these "children" if they lived on reservations.[1]

Col. John Chivington

During the 1850s when emigrants were crossing the continent on their way to California and Oregon, many politicians demanded that the Plains Indians, including Sioux, Lakota, Arapaho, Cheyenne, and other tribes, be pushed out of the way to clear paths to the West.

There was little concern about depriving Indians of their hunting grounds and taking their land.

In 1851 government officials had summoned thousands of Plains Indians to a council at Fort Laramie, Wyoming. By bringing wagonloads of food and gifts, they induced a few chiefs who could not read to accept a treaty. It recognized the right of the United States to build roads and establish military posts on the plains. The treaty also designated boundaries that confined each tribe within specific areas. This limited hunting grounds. To compensate, the government promised to protect the Indians from white men, and to provide food, and supplies worth $50,00 a year for fifty years.[2]

Many Indians didn't know about the treaty. Those who did refused to be hemmed in by borders, for they were accustomed to chasing game across the wide expanses of the plains. They were also in a fury because money that was supposed to be spent on food and supplies for them was pocketed by dishonest federal agents. As a result, small groups of embittered braves gave vent to their anger by attacking emigrants, trappers, wagon trains, and government surveyors. United States soldiers retaliated by killing Indians, including those who had never hurt anyone.

Another treaty, made in 1861 at Fort Wise, Colorado, forced these same Indians to give up all the territory that had been promised to them at Fort Laramie. They were moved to a miserable piece of land bounded by Sand Creek and the Arkansas River in Colorado. Only a few chiefs signed this treaty, and some of those who did declared later that they had been tricked. Why would they give up territory that the United States government had promised was theirs forever?

Why would they agree to settle on arid land far from their usual hunting grounds? What recourse did they have against cheating officials who offered near-starvation rations of food? The United States government had doomed them to poverty, hunger, and despair. As a result, they attacked whites, not only to give vent to their anger, but also to obtain food.

Even though attacks against whites had been random, John Evans, the governor of Colorado Territory, wanted to wage war against the Plains Indians. Col. John Chivington, Evans's military commander, was also eager for action, especially because he had political ambitions, and he was sure that killing "redskins" would enhance his image.

Indians and government officials met at Fort Laramie, Wyoming.

Pawnee Scouts
at a railroad
station

Both he and Governor Evans refused to hear pleas for peace made by Cheyenne chiefs.

On November 28, 1864, Chivington and a regiment of volunteers attacked Cheyenne lodges at Sand Creek. His instructions were, "Kill and scalp all, big and little."[3] An American flag given by President Lincoln flew over Chief Black Kettle's tipi, but this sign of friendship was ignored. Chivington's men were in a fighting frenzy. They scalped and killed men, women, boys, girls, and babies indiscriminately. At least 150 Cheyenne were slaughtered.

Although many white people were horrified, some people in Denver approved the massacre at Sand Creek.

Hailed as heroes, volunteer fighters appeared at a theater. Audiences cheered and applauded them when they strung grisly Indian scalps across the stage.

The brutality of the Sand Creek atrocities fomented anti-white hatred. By 1865, hundreds of Sioux, Cheyenne, and Arapaho warriors had banded together. They burned ranches, attacked stage coaches, destroyed telegraph lines, plundered wagon trains, and killed "palefaces."

In February 1865 Gen. Grenville Dodge headed military operations in Kansas, and in the Nebraska, Colorado, Utah, and Dakota Territories. He commanded army units, but most of his troops consisted of 6,000 ex-Confederate soldiers who had been captured by the Union Army. Rather than continue miserable existences in northern prisoner-of-war camps, they chose to fight Indians.[4] Dodge also hired Pawnee scouts, who were eager for war against their long-standing enemies, the Sioux and Cheyenne.

When Vice President Andrew Johnson became President after Lincoln's assassination in April 1865, government policy regarding Indians changed drastically. Four years of Civil War had caused enough bloodshed, and President Johnson saw no need for fighting an Indian war that might last for years. He estimated that military operations would drain the national treasury of 15 to 50 million dollars. Even though raids killed some workers, Indian attacks really did not slow or stop railroad construction. Therefore, the president rejected the requests by Generals Grant, Sherman, and Dodge for additional troops. President Johnson suspected that these officers deliberately provoked Indians to fight. Because he objected to their aggressive army tactics, he issued orders reducing the number of soldiers by more than half, to 2,500.[5]

Dodge was shocked. He had 3,500 miles of mail and telegraph lines to protect. "There are 25,000 Indians on the plains, north and south," he reported. "We need more troops, not less."[6] As a result, frontier soldiers who policed enormous

A clash between the
Army and the Indians

areas did not have to fight many battles against the Indians.

On December 21, 1866, after Dodge became the Union Pacific's chief engineer, the Army suffered one of its worst defeats. Capt. William Fetterman was responsible. This egotistical braggart belittled the danger of native warriors. He boasted that he needed only 80 men to help him whip "the whole Sioux nation."[7] Fetterman was elated when his superior, Colonel Carrington, sent him out with 80 soldiers so that he could rescue woodcutters from an Indian raiding party. He was told to return to headquarters at Fort Phil Kearny, Wyoming, immediately after saving the woodcutters. He had explicit instructions not to pursue the Indians. However, eager to prove his mettle as a fighter, and contemptuous of his superior officer's nonaggressive position, Fetterman deliberately ignored orders. After rescuing the woodcutting party, he went after the Indians. He and his men galloped into an ambush, where more than a thousand braves attacked. All of his eighty soldiers were killed. Fetterman shot himself, rather than be taken prisoner.

This disastrous defeat for the Army—and meaningful victory for the Indians—took place only 60 miles from Union Pacific construction workers. It was truly frightening for the crew and very dismaying for Durant. While workers feared for their lives, Durant worried that news of the defeat would discourage investors.

General Sherman was enraged when he learned of the Fetterman disaster. He was in a fury especially because of the White House peace policy toward Indians. "We must act with vindictive earnestness against the Sioux," he wrote, "even to their extermination, men, women, and children."[8]

Attacks Against the Iron Horse

The Plains Indians saw tracks being laid on hunting grounds that treaties had promised were to be theirs forever. They watched trains whose clangs and shrieks frightened away their game. They witnessed the wanton slaying of their sacred buffalo by sportsmen who enjoyed shooting, then left the animals to rot. Threatened with starvation, extinction, or incarceration on loathsome reservations, they fought back.

One group of Sioux tried to capture an iron horse that was chugging and puffing across the prairies. Using a 40-foot rope that their medicine man had imbued with magic, they stretched it across the tracks, expecting to hold back the metal monster. Unfortunately, before the rope broke, two braves who held fast were pulled under the locomotive's wheels and killed.

Construction crews were protected by soldiers who

camped within sight of workers' tents. Therefore, Indians chose to strike at small isolated groups. On May 25, 1867, they suddenly leaped from the cover of tall prairie grass and killed five tracklayers. That same day other warriors killed four graders, and then they deliberately galloped alongside Casement's boarding train, defiantly shouting war whoops. Three government commissioners who had come to inspect construction were on board at that time. They shouldered guns to help workers fight, but by the time they took aim the enemy had vanished. Dodge exclaimed, "We've got to clean the damn Indians out or give up building the Union Pacific. The government may make its choice."[9]

Upon returning to Washington the three commissioners provided eyewitness testimony that Indians were a menace to progress. As commander of the Military Division of the West, General Sherman dispatched infantry and cavalry units to guard Union Pacific workers. He told them, "The more we can kill this year, the less will have to be killed the next war, for the more I see of these Indians the more convinced I am that they all have to be killed or be maintained as a species of paupers."[10]

The number of attacks against the railroad decreased, but there were some disheartening losses. The body of one engineer was discovered with nineteen arrows and five bullet wounds, and a chief surveyor died after being shot in the stomach by a mounted Sioux fighter. These were token reprisals by Indians who were being hunted as though they were animals.

Plains Indians shot arrows at trains but didn't cause any major damages. It took a small group of impoverished Cheyenne, who had escaped north from Kansas, to destroy an Iron Horse.

Cheyenne chief Turkey Foot and a small group of braves had fled to Nebraska, far from the onslaught of U.S. soldiers who had burned their village. These Indians had never seen or heard of a railroad. Porcupine, who was one of their braves, recalled that when his group first sighted a locomotive, they remarked that "it smoked like a white man's pipe, when he was smoking." He continued, "Now the white people have taken all we had and have made us poor and we ought to do something. In these big wagons that go on this metal road, there must be things that are valuable—perhaps clothing. If we could throw these wagons off the iron then run and break them open, we should find out what was in them and could take whatever might be useful to us."[11] Homeless, poor, and bitter about their plight, they uprooted rails, tied them together with telegraph wires they had yanked down, and waited for their puffing, iron enemy. Because of the broken telegraph lines, six repairmen rode a handcar to the troublespot. The handcar derailed when it reached the broken tracks. The Cheyenne killed five.[12]

Shortly after this derailment, the Cheyenne were startled by dazzling lights. At first they thought these were stars that had descended from heaven. Then they realized they were looking at the headlights of a down-to-earth Union Pacific freight train heading their way. The uprooted tracks caused it to crash.[13]

The Cheyenne broke into the freight cars and collected loot. They found whiskey, which made them drunk, and assorted items that they used as though they were party decorations. The warriors donned ladies' bonnets, draped velvets and ruffles around their bodies, adorned themselves with ribbons, and tied long lengths of calico to their horses' tails. Before angry "palefaces" arrived from Plum Creek, Nebraska, they had galloped away.

This was the first time natives had wrecked a train. A small band of homeless Cheyenne had shown others how to derail cars and attack their occupants. In September 1868, Indians wrecked a Union Pacific train by prying up rails. Passengers using rifles kept on overhead racks forced their

Indians destroying Union Pacific tracks

attackers to retreat. The locomotive's fireman, who was thrown against the firebox and burned to death when the engine crashed, was the only fatality.

Sherman had insisted that no mission was more urgent than clearing out Indians between the Platte and Arkansas Rivers. He wanted to open the way for Union Pacific rails. Once rails were set, iron horses would frighten and drive away the giant herds of buffalo, and without the buffalo, the Plains Indians would be deprived of animals that were vital to their way of life.

Sacred Buffalo

Plains Indians were completely dependent upon buffalo for their material and spiritual well-being. The animals provided them with meat, both fresh and dried, for year-round use; hides for clothing, bedding, tents, and ropes; bones for tools and weapons; sinews for bowstrings, thread, and twine; hoofs for glue; horns for cups, ladles, and spoons. Even the animals' dung, when dried into chips, was used for fuel.

Buffalo were viewed as a sacred blessing, worthy of worship. The creatures were the main focus of religious rites. Through prayers, dances, and incantations, tribes hoped to lure the migrating animals to their hunting grounds. Skulls of the beasts were placed in many locations, based upon the belief that buffalo would seek out these "white-faced companions." Without buffalo, tribes would suffer.

During the 1850s, there had been a brisk trade between traders and tribes for buffalo robes that had been prepared by Indian women. By 1867 a tremendous number of hunters had set out to kill buffalo for profit. Back East, skins were in demand not only for clothes and blankets, but also for wall decorations, carriage covers, and sleigh seats. Elastic buffalo hide made excellent belting for factory machinery, and the

FOLLOWING PAGES: Shooting buffalo was a popular sport for some Eastern tourists.

Sacred circles of buffalo skulls were seen on the plains.

ground-up bones were used for fertilizer, for processing refined sugar, and for manufacturing bone china. The railroad provided a new means of transporting huge quantities of bulky skins and bones to big cities.

Outings to hunt buffalo just for sport became the rage for Europeans as well as Americans looking for adventure. These hunters found it easy to shoot into buffalo herds at close range. They would kill enough to boast about, and then leave the carcasses to rot on the prairies.

The Union Pacific Railroad cashed in on the craze by advertising sight-seeing excursions that included buffalo hunts. On these excursions, passengers took shots at buffalo from the windows of a moving train. The dead and injured animals were left behind as the train moved on. Killing buffalo to feed railroad crews added to the slaughter.[14]

Construction workers wanted buffalo destroyed because these beasts damaged roadbeds and tracks by trampling over them. The animals also uprooted telegraph poles when they used them during spring as scratching posts to rub shedding hairs off their thick winter fur.

Army officers supported buffalo hunting largely because the extinction of these animals would force Indians to live on reservations. In September 1867 General Sherman told the Plains Indians: "Our people East hardly think of what you call 'war' here, but if they make up their minds to fight you, they will come out as thick as a herd of buffalo, and if you continue fighting you will be killed. We advise you for the best. We now offer you this: choose your own homes and live like white men, and we will help you all you want.... We will be kind to you if you keep the peace, but if you won't listen to reason, we are ordered to make war upon you."[15]

When there were too few buffalo to sustain them, the Plains Indians were forced to give up their lands.

When buffalo became scarce, many Plains Indians had to move to reservations.

8 Gaining Ground

Gambling joints attracted
crowds of customers.

RUFFIANS WHO ACCOMPANIED the Union Pacific and rowdy workmen were the real "wild savages" of the Great Plains. Drinking, brawling, and occasionally murdering their way across America, they introduced their version of civilization into Indian country.

It Was Wild

As construction pushed west, work gangs set up temporary tent cities. Gamblers, saloon keepers, dance-hall operators, prostitutes, drifters, and outlaws followed the tracks, mak-

Shootout

ing each a "sin stop" that earned the name "hell on wheels"—
a term used by writer Samuel Bowles after he had visited
several of these settlements.[1] When rails were laid about 60
miles beyond an encampment canvas tents and equipment
were reloaded on flatcars, brought forward, and set up again as
recreation centers for construction crews. Usually these places
were deserted when the railroaders moved. In many instances,
however, a canvas settlement grew to become a large city,
such as Cheyenne, Wyoming.

In November 1866 North Platte, Nebraska, became the
first permanent settlement. Within three weeks, a brick roundhouse for 40 locomotives, a hotel, and 18 other buildings
were erected. Gambling joints and drinking saloons in shacks
and tents quickly had a steady stream of customers. Only two
months after North Platte was founded, Union Pacific trains
shuttled daily to and from Omaha, 290 miles away. A traveler who visited North Platte reported that tradesmen, miners,
and soldiers joined railroad gangs that were "having a good
time, gambling, drinking, and shooting each other."[2]

By 1867 North Platte was called merely "a quaint frontier hamlet" when compared with Julesburg, Nebraska. Julesburg became known as "The Wickedest City in America." Henry Stanley, reporter for the *New York Herald*, wrote that "there are men here who would murder a fellow creature for five dollars.... Not a day passes but a dead body is found somewhere in the vicinity with pockets rifled of their contents."[3] Dance-halls and saloons made nights noisy and lively; hangovers and funerals made mornings deadly quiet.

The situation aggravated Dodge who, in addition to being chief engineer, was authorized to sell land for the Union Pacific. He had mapped out town lots for Julesburg and anticipated selling them at high prices. When gamblers took over property and refused to pay for land owned by the railroad, "General Jack" Casement followed Dodge's orders. He marched into town with 200 men, fired into a crowd, and killed a number of people. Casement took Dodge to a cemetery and boasted, "They all died in their boots and

Saloon scene

Julesburg has been quiet since."[4] "The Wickedest Town in the World" never amounted to anything, anyway. After five months, when the railroad moved farther west, it was as still as its graveyard.

The town of Sidney, Nebraska, the next stopover, was so dangerous that passengers were not allowed to go outside when the train stopped at the station to unload freight. Travelers didn't even feel safe sitting in their seats because hoodlums thought it was hilarious to pepper passenger cars with bullets.

Bear River City, Wyoming

By July 1867 construction workers had advanced to Cheyenne, Wyoming. Dodge made it an important Union Pacific depot. He was disgusted by the many wild, rough inhabitants who had set up their saloons, brothels, and betting parlors at Union Pacific stopovers. Dodge called Cheyenne the gambling capital of the world, and wrote that "like Julesburg...it will be a second hell."[5] To halt the mayhem, the local magistrate was said to fine any man who fired a gun $10, "whether he hit or missed."[6] A log cabin that served as a one-room jailhouse was so overcrowded that to make space for more prisoners jailbirds were periodically let out and ordered to leave town fast or be hanged. Murders were so commonplace that the town's newspaper ran a daily column called "LAST NIGHT'S SHOOTINGS."

Ruffians who came to Cheyenne seized lots owned by the railroad and threatened to shoot any Union Pacific agent who demanded payment for property. When they refused to budge, Dodge called in government troops, who tore down their shacks and ran the squatters out of town.

Within a year, by 1868, the city started to show signs of respectability. It opened a public school, erected a church, and officials forced one of its theaters to clean up the language of its songs and skits so that respectable ladies could attend without being shocked. Law-abiding citizens made Cheyenne a thriving city, but crimes continued to be prominently featured in the town's newspaper.

In April 1868 a Union Pacific land agent waited at Laramie, Wyoming, for the construction gang and its followers. Within one week he sold 200 town lots to gamblers, saloon keepers, traders, and squatters who kept moving on with Union Pacific work trains. This time buyers made enormous profits, for Laramie became a permanent railroad town. Bowles said it was an ideal spot for "the weary traveler, the sportsman [who liked trout fishing], or the invalid to linger for days and weeks."[7]

Energized by bonuses, workmen sprinted ahead so speedily that by early August 1868, having completed 695 miles of track, they set up another roaring town, Benton, Wyoming. It was located in a scorching desert. Water, which had to be carried by wagon from a river three miles away, was used sparingly because it cost more than whiskey. Washing was considered unnecessary. Desert dust coated everything and everybody. Bowles called Benton "by day disgusting, by night dangerous; almost everybody dirty, many filthy, and with marks of lowest vice; averaging a murder a day."[8]

Despite the dreadful location, Dodge sold $17,000 worth of lots to buyers who were convinced that Benton would become a booming city. After two months the place was deserted. Only trash, broken-down shanties, and a cemetery filled with the victims of bar brawls and gunfights remained.

As the railroad rolled along, many more Wild West towns developed. Bear River City near the Utah border was reputedly the worst of all. On November 19, 1868, outlaws on a tear burned the town's jail and wrecked its newspaper office. At least 14 railroad workers were killed and dozens more wounded.

During 1868, when rails were laid across Wyoming and parts of Utah, the Union Pacific advanced at a speed that exceeded a mile a day, making tracks that altogether stretched 982 miles. Cheyenne, Laramie, and other towns along the line were creations of the Union Pacific. They owed their founding and their growth to the railroad.

Workers hired by the company heading east, the Central Pacific Railroad, also spawned tent cities that existed for a short time, then disappeared, and sometimes reappeared as the iron horse continued to race eastward. A California newspaper reported, "Camp equipage, work shops, boarding house offices, and in fact the big settlement literally took up its bed and walked.... A busy town of 5,000 inhabitants in the morning was a deserted village site at night."[9]

Most Central Pacific stopovers could not be compared with the Union Pacific's settlements. California construction boss Strobridge loathed liquor. He made sure that any place selling whiskey was quickly put out of business. "A saloon would spring up in a tent once in a while," he noted, "when a crowd would rush it and break bottles and heads with pick handles, and the good red liquor ran like rain."[10] There were, however, places such as Wadsworth and Reno that became rowdy hangouts frequented by fortune hunters going to and from mines in Nevada and California.

Land Bargains

The Pacific Railroad Acts gave both the Central Pacific and Union Pacific enormous amounts of land that they could break up into small lots and sell. The government expected to enrich the nation by expanding settlements throughout the country. The railroad companies realized that their profits depended upon passengers, markets, and freight. Tracks to destinations in deserted areas would derail them financially. They had to populate whistle-stops by selling parcels of property at any price.

The federal government shared ownership of lands near the railroads. By law, acreage was parceled out in a checker-

A small box-like shack could be used to establish a claim.

FULL STEAM AHEAD

board pattern: a square mile belonging to the railroad alternated with a square mile owned by the United States.

Anxious to populate the West, Congress passed the Homestead Act in 1862, the same year the first Pacific Railroad Act had been passed. The Homestead Act offered 160 acres free to any adult citizen or any foreigner who intended to become a citizen. However, to qualify, a homesteader was obligated to build a dwelling on the land, pass one night there at least once every six months, and spend five years improving the property. By law no person was allowed to own more than one homestead plot. The government didn't want rich individuals or big corporations controlling vast tracts of land.

Shopkeepers and businessmen who could get hold of land near railroad stops where towns might thrive were in the best position to take advantage of the government free-land offer—if they weren't victimized by land sharks out to cheat them. There were con men who showed Easterners the map of a city in the prairies that had shopping areas, churches, schools, and theaters. When customers who had bought lots arrived to take over their property, they found a few broken-down shacks—or just wide open spaces near a prairie dog town.

The Union Pacific hired its own promoters to pump up business. Elaborate brochures were circulated throughout the United States, and in Europe, too, extolling fertile land made available by railroads. One writer declared that the entire population of Europe could be sustained on the prairies. "Throughout the vast plains," he noted, "heretofore occupied by savages or lying vacant in solitary grandeur a new and attractive expanse will now be opened presenting the advantages of safety, fertility and ready access which will make it

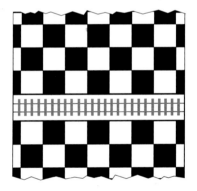

Because of the railroad, farmers could move West. Acreage was parceled out in a checkerboard pattern. The black squares represent lands given to the railroad. The white squares represent lands kept by the government or sold to others.

This pamphlet, publicized in Sweden, lured immigrants to Nebraska.

inviting and remunerative [profitable] to the immigrant." Readers were urged to apply for land quickly, because when the railroad was finished prices of property would skyrocket.[11] Anyone expecting to establish new homes in the West could buy a railroad ticket at a bargain price. Families seeking a better life endured sitting on train benches without backs as they traveled in crude passenger cars over roughly graded Union Pacific tracks.

Railroad officials were intent upon filling up empty lands in a hurry, not only to make money by selling property, but also to create markets that would guarantee freight and passenger business.

In October 1867 George Train, the Union Pacific's great booster, invited 200 newspapermen, including some from England and Belgium, to participate in the Editorial Rocky Mountain Excursion. Like the successful Excursion of 1866, this trip included banquets, buffalo hunts, stops at prairie dog towns, and performances featuring "wild Indians." At Omaha, George Train showed off the 5,000 city lots he owned. On the plains he boasted that the soil was so fertile "if you tickle it with a spade it laughs with potatoes." At Columbus, Nebraska, he bragged about his own investments there, insisting that the town had "magnificent agricultural surroundings."[12] Near Julesburg, Nebraska, reporters were issued hiking shoes so that they could march to the end of the track and watch railroad crews at work.

Two hundred enthusiastic newspaper writers filled their notebooks with sentences applauding the Union Pacific and praising the value of land on the plains. The Editorial Rocky Mountain Excursion had been a great show, and it received rave reviews.

Excursions and handbills to promote the West continued to influence settlers. New fictions replaced an old myth about the plains being a Great American Desert. "Rain follows the plow" became a popular slogan. Some promoters declared that an increase in population caused rainfall. Others spread the senseless belief that steam from locomotives moistened and enriched the soil.

Land became valuable only after railways were built. Therefore, the great rush to establish new homes, farms, ranches, and businesses in the West did not take place until the 1870s and 1880s, after the Central Pacific and Union Pacific Railroads had been completed. These and other railroads brought people who cultivated the countryside and established thriving cities.[13]

Europeans arriving in Lincoln, Nebraska

Newspapers could be set up quickly before towns were developed.
The smallest settlement often had its own newspaper.

9 The Great Race

IN JANUARY 1868 stockholders of the Union Pacific held a meeting in New York City. They were very disturbed because work gangs of the Central Pacific, having finished laying tracks over the High Sierra, were racing across a flat Nevada desert. Their rival was gaining ground that could belong to the Union Pacific! Therefore, Durant and other investors insisted that Dodge order his men to advance quickly, despite bitter winter weather, at "no matter what the cost."[1] Laborers willingly worked nights and Sundays for extra pay.

To expedite shipping freight from the East, a temporary railroad bridge was laid on top of the Missouri River's ice at Omaha. Surveyors in Utah's Wasatch Mountains used snowshoes and sleighs to travel over snow so high it reached the tops of telegraph poles. Track gangs made bonfires in below zero temperatures to stave off frostbite. Lacking timber, they burned valuable railroad ties. Trackmen laid lines on ice and snow, not worrying about spring thaws that would cause rails to separate from the ground and result in train accidents. At

FOLLOWING PAGES:
Building a bridge at
Green River, Wyoming

one place tracks on a frozen stream bank were so insecure that the rails, together with a train, slid into the water.

During 1868 and 1869, rushing to race ahead, both Central Pacific and Union Pacific gangs put together rickety, flimsy bridges over rivers and ravines. At many places, instead of tunnels, they hastily made roads that spiraled up and down mountains. Tracks and trestles were so shoddy and dangerous that hundreds of miles would eventually have to be redone at enormous costs. Curved roadbeds would have to be straightened, rough grades made smooth, and bridges rebuilt.

Eastern newspapers whipped up excitement and increased their circulation by publishing daily bulletins about the length of track the Union Pacific completed. Journalists from New York, Chicago, Philadelphia, Pittsburgh, Baltimore, Cincinnati, and many other cities went to Wyoming during the summer and fall of 1868 to wire reports from the Union Pacific construction front and to glean whatever information they could from travelers about the Central Pacific's progress. Readers, riveted with suspense, avidly followed news about America's great railroad race, as though they were checking out championship sports scores.

Help From Mormons

To hurry ahead, leaders of both companies hoped to hire additional manpower and buy supplies and provisions from Mormons who had settled in Utah Territory.

Members of the Church of Jesus Christ of Latter-day Saints, commonly called Mormons, had been persecuted because their religious beliefs differed from those of other Christians. To escape hostility, they first moved from New York to Ohio, then to Missouri, and from there to Illinois, where their leader Joseph Smith was murdered by a mob. Under the inspiring leadership of Brigham Young, followers set out upon a journey of a thousand miles to find a place where they could live in peace. In 1847 the first group of 148 Mormons settled in a desert beside the Great Salt Lake, on land they were sure no one else wanted. They planted crops and irrigated parched ground with water from a nearby creek. Their promised land, isolated from prejudiced mobs, had been found.

Thousands of Mormon converts from the eastern United States and Europe willingly endured the hardships of travel for the safety and security waiting for them in their "Kingdom of God." In 1849 a missionary service supplied money to pay converts' travel expenses. Under Brigham Young's leadership, Mormons created a remarkable oasis in a desert. They built irrigation ditches that carried water from mountain streams not only to farms but also to household gardens within Salt Lake City. Flowers, fruits, and vegetables were abundant. Cattle grazed on lush pastures; corn and wheat flourished on expansive fields. Salt Lake City became a business hub with traders, shopkeepers, and skilled laborers. By 1860 more than 40,000 pioneers had built over 150 settlements, and by 1868 Utah's Mormon population was close to 80,000.

By the spring of 1868 iron horses from the Central Pacific and Union Pacific companies were heading toward Mormon territory. A Union Pacific engineer traveled to Salt Lake City where he negotiated a two-million-dollar contract with Brigham Young for 4,000 Mormon construction workers. The agreement specified grading, tunneling, and bridge building in Utah, from Echo Canyon to Ogden. As a bonus, Mormons who used Union Pacific trains were to be charged reduced rates.

Hiring Mormon labor and monopolizing its freight business proved so important that Central Pacific's Leland Stanford left the comforts of his California home and stayed in Salt Lake City until he had negotiated a one-million-dollar contract with Brigham Young for an unspecified number of laborers to grade

Brigham Young

roadbeds from the Nevada border to Weber Canyon, Utah.

When both the Union Pacific and Central Pacific agreements were made, Brigham Young assumed that Salt Lake City would become a major depot. The Mormon leader was told after the contracts were signed that both Central Pacific and Union Pacific surveyors had concluded that routes to Salt Lake City were too difficult. Instead, the two lines would pass through Ogden, Utah, 40 miles away. Brigham Young was in a fury, until Dodge promised that the Union Pacific would eventually help Young build a line linking Salt Lake City with Ogden.[2] A transcontinental railroad within reasonable wagon-distance would greatly benefit the Utah Mormons. They would be able to

Ogden, Utah

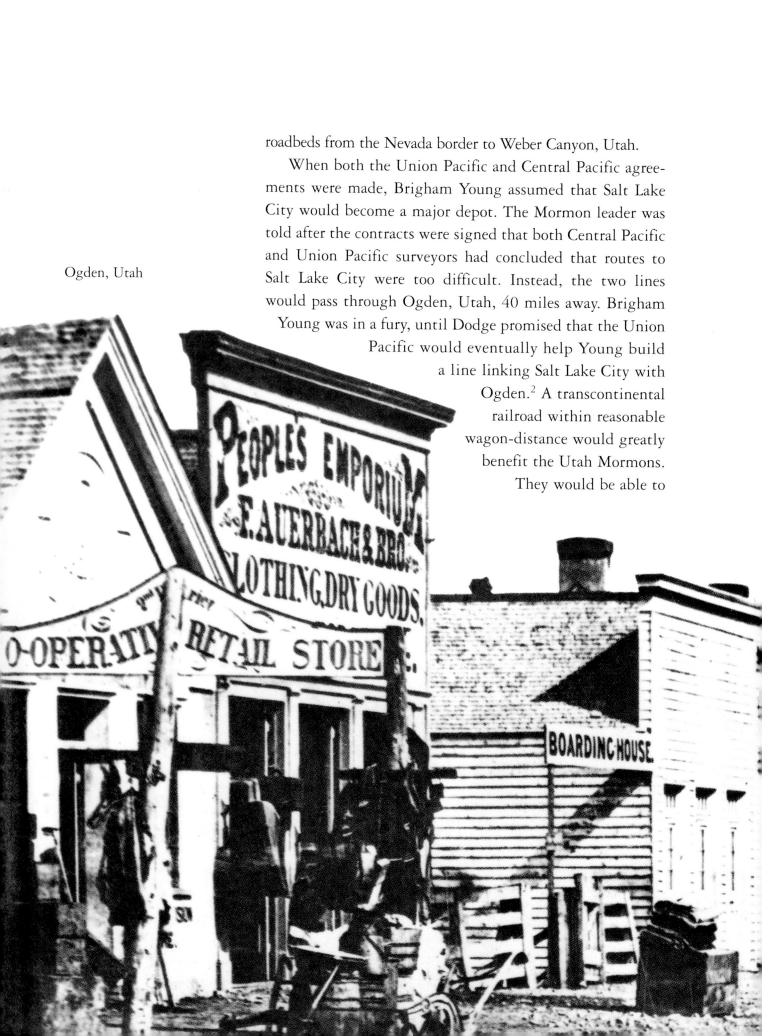

export their products, as well as import machinery and tools from manufacturers in the East.

Church elders encouraged railroad building. They realized that trains would not only improve their economy, but also increase their numbers. Converts would no longer have to endure the hardships of long overland pilgrimages on foot or by wagon. The elders were dismayed, however, when rowdy workman came to the Salt Lake area. Cursing, smoking, drinking, gambling, and fighting offended them. They wondered whether they would not have been better off living in isolation; the railroad exposed their children to evil ways.

However, most families agreed it was best to get the job done as quickly as possible so that the rough-necks would leave and the Mormon boys working for the Union Pacific could return home.

Both Central Pacific and Union Pacific grading crews

were located as many as 150 miles ahead of tracklayers. They worked on the north side of the Great Salt Lake—and dug parallel roadbeds within sight of each other! This wasteful work was deliberately sanctioned by the stockholders of both companies who were determined to avoid a meeting point as long as possible. They each gleefully collected $32,000 per mile for 290 miles of unnecessary, duplicate road building.

In the mountains of Utah, Strobridge's Chinese crews found themselves working less than a hundred feet away from the Union Pacific's road gangs. According to Dodge, "there was much ill-feeling between them."[3] Rivalry turned vicious. First, the Union Pacific workers threw clods of frozen dirt at the Chinese. Then they attacked with pickaxes. Finally, they set off explosions that killed some of the Chinese. To retaliate, the Chinese set off blasts that caused an avalanche of dirt and rocks. Several men were buried alive. According to Dodge, "This brought about a truce at once.... There was no further trouble."[4]

It was obvious from news reports that one of America's most historic events—connecting the railroads—could take place at any time. Although many journalists touted the train race with pride, some called the event corrupt. They accused Central Pacific and Union Pacific officials of being land-grabbers who were not concerned about quality construction, but only about making "the largest profit with the least possible risk."[5] Reacting to this bad publicity, congressmen planned an investigation of the parallel roadbeds that wasted government money. They were also troubled that there was *still* no meeting point. On March 4, 1869, the very day he became President, Ulysses S. Grant warned the railroad companies that the government would withhold future payments unless the directors determined where their lines would join.

Threats from the White House and Congress got action. The Union Pacific's Durant, his engineer, Dodge, and the Central Pacific's Huntington, went into an all-night huddle

on April 9, 1869. They agreed to join tracks at Promontory Summit, a barren spot north of the Great Salt Lake—690 track miles from Sacramento, 1,086 track miles from Omaha. The next day, Congress passed a resolution making Promontory Summit "the common terminus...at which point the rails shall meet and connect and form one continuous line."[6]

Plans were made for nationwide celebrations. The transcontinental railroad was about to become a reality.

As rails neared Promontory Summit, rival crews of the Union Pacific and Central Pacific were grading and blasting near each other.

10 A Grand Celebration

BEFORE THE HISTORIC JOINING of the rails took place, the Central Pacific's pushy boss, Charlie Crocker, decided to capture the public's attention with his own show. He had been out of sorts because the Union Pacific had received more publicity from newspapers than the Central Pacific. It had grabbed the limelight, especially after workmen had laid eight and a half miles of track in one day. Crocker couldn't resist an opportunity to show off his own men's prowess. He announced that April 28, 1869, would become known as "Ten Mile Day." To guarantee success, he handpicked his best men and promised to pay them four days' wages for one day's work. Reporters, photographers, Army officers, and tourists showed up to watch this race against time. Jack Casement and other Union Pacific men were there, too, hoping Crocker's show would fail and stop short in its tracks.

Crocker's marathon started at dawn with the screech of a train whistle. Within eight minutes, 16 cars loaded with enough iron rails and material for two miles were unloaded, then thrown on to handcars that were pulled by horses to

A simple sign marks an
all-time record.

FOLLOWING PAGES:
Camp Victory, Utah, near
Promontory Summit.
Strobridge is standing on a
flatcar in the center fore-
ground, in a dark suit.

Promontory Summit, Utah, became the meeting place of the Central Pacific and Union Pacific.

waiting crews. Spikes, bolts, and rails were delivered at breakneck speed. At the end of the track eight burly Irishmen set rails. Each rail was 30 feet long and weighed 560 pounds. Additional supplies were delivered as cars rolled up to the construction front, so that the crew moved forward at the average rate of 1 mile an hour. By noon 6 miles of track had been laid, and workers were allowed to halt for a 1-hour lunch break. By 7 p.m. they had set a new record: 10 miles and 56 feet in 12 hours. Central Pacific's champions had put down 25,800 ties, laid 3,520 rails, used 28,160 spikes, and turned 14,080 bolts. Each of the 8 rail setters had lifted 264,000 pounds of iron that day—totaling over 2 million pounds of heavy metal.

Crocker was overjoyed. He had timed the event perfectly. The rival railroad couldn't beat the Central Pacific's Ten Mile Day for this reason: Union Pacific construction crews were less than nine miles from Promontory Summit. They didn't have the ten miles needed to duplicate the feat.[1]

Union Pacific officials were on their way to Promontory Summit when their engine was stopped by railroad ties piled on the track. Terrified passengers were thrown from their seats when the train made a jarring halt.

Hundreds of angry Union Pacific workmen were outside,

shouting, and demanding back pay. They uncoupled Durant's car, switched it to a side track, chained the wheels to the rails, and made Durant and an important Union Pacific director, John Duff, their prisoners. Guests were told to get out and move to another car.

Durant and Duff were captives of Union Pacific construction workers who had not received wages for months. Durant was warned that if he didn't telegraph for money right away, he would end up in the mountains eating sagebrush and salted horse.

Durant hastily scribbled a note to Oliver Ames in Boston. Members of the mob rushed to the telegraph station at nearby Piedmont to dispatch it. When Ames received the telegram, he prepared to send a wire to Dodge, who was in Salt Lake City, urging him to organize a military rescue party. But the Boston telegraph operator, in sympathy with the workers, refused to transmit Ames's wire. A second telegram was sent to warn Ames that if money for back pay was not received quickly, workers would stop Union Pacific trains from running.

The company had spent so much on supplies that it did not have funds to meet payrolls. The Ames brothers had to use their own money to free Durant and Duff. Through banks in Cheyenne and Laramie, funds were rushed to the scene 48 hours after the men had been kidnapped. As soon as they were released, they hoped to hurry ahead. The great joining of the rails had been scheduled for Saturday, May 8.

On May 5 the group was stalled again at Devil's Gate, 13 miles from Ogden. Heavy rains had weakened a rickety Union Pacific railroad bridge that had been built 50 feet above a canyon's stream. It had to be shored up before it collapsed. Durant himself directed repairs, but even after 200 workmen reinforced the bridge, the engineer refused to risk his life riding a heavy locomotive across the structure. However, he assured Durant that the bridge would support lighter passenger coaches. Each car was then uncoupled and shoved by the locomotive so that it rolled across the bridge to the other side. Terrified passengers sat inside their coaches as they moved across the bridge in the dark of night. Once across, they were stranded without a locomotive, but rescue was soon on the way. One of the workers tapped a nearby telegraph line and wired the station at Ogden to send help. Passengers were relieved when Engine Number 119 arrived to pull their train to Promontory Summit.

Durant and his guests had endured a miserable, frightening 48-hour delay at Devil's Gate. They didn't reach Promontory Summit until late Sunday. Ceremonies had to be postponed until Monday, May 10.

Leland Stanford set out from Sacramento on Wednesday, May 5, expecting to participate in gala celebrations at Promontory Summit three days later.

Stanford was the only member of the Big Four who would attend the ceremonies. Rather than travel to a dismal desert location, Huntington preferred to conduct business in New York. Crocker and Hopkins remained in California.

Stanford's special train had only two cars. One was

FACING PAGE:
Conference in an ornate private car. Durant is seated third from left.

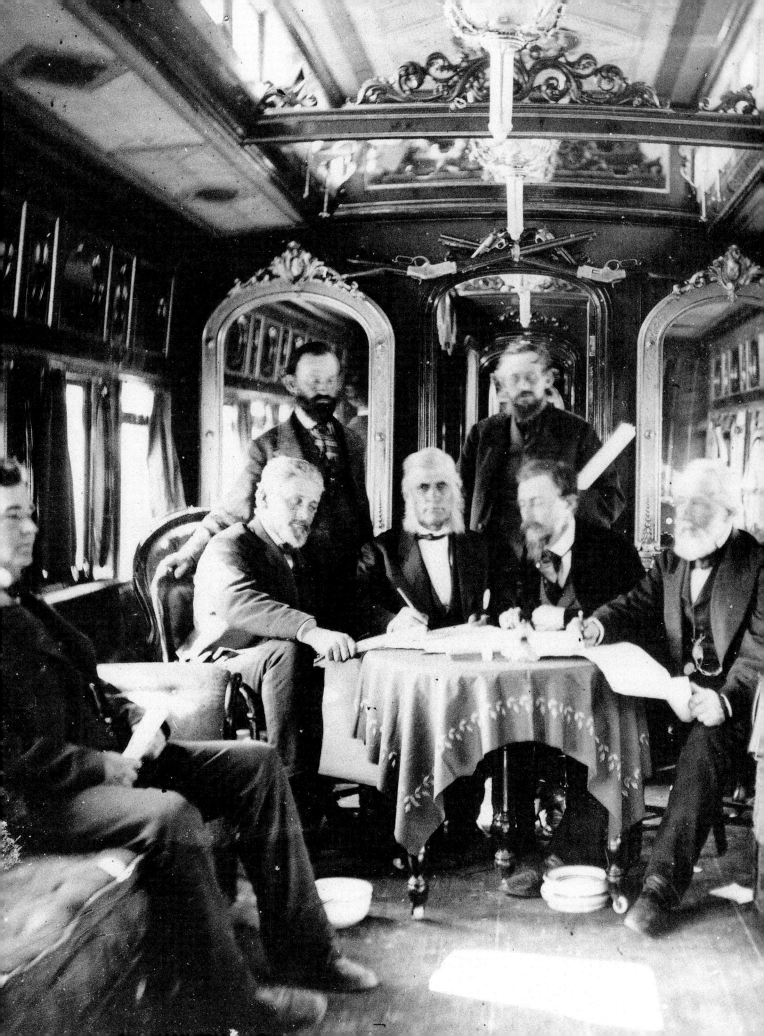

Poster advertising the grand opening of the transcontinental railroad

equipped with a kitchen, dining room, lounge, and beds for ten people. The other carried live chickens, sides of beef, assorted fruits, groceries, and an enormous stock of champagne. Spirits were dampened by days of constant rain and bumpy roadbeds that made one guest feel as though he was "being tossed in a blanket."[2] The California party arrived at Promontory Summit on Friday, May 7, only to be told that the Easterners would be days late. It rained incessantly the entire weekend.

Promontory Summit was a horrid place to stage a ceremony marking an event that the *New York Times* hailed as "the completion of the greatest enterprise ever yet undertaken...the greatest marvel in the whole history of civil engineering."[3] The town didn't have any permanent buildings—just tents, some with wooden fronts. These were on one miserable street that was set back only a few yards from the railroad tracks. Workers and visitors spent time in saloons there and at the the nearby tent towns of Deadfall and Last Chance. According to reports, 24 men had been murdered in these whiskey camps during the previous 25 days.

There were champagne parties in Stanford's luxurious car, but these couldn't cure boredom and exasperation. To while away the time, Stanford visited a Union Pacific construction camp and went sightseeing in the mountains and on the shores of the Great Salt Lake.

In California people were having a grand time. They had not been told about the delay, and even if they had known, it would have been difficult to postpone planned celebrations. Delegations of dignitaries and trainloads of tourists pulled into Sacramento to enjoy parties, watch parades, hear bands, and see fireworks. In San Francisco church bells rang, steam whistles shrieked, guns banged, and cannons boomed, to make noise about the news that rails had been linked—two days before the event actually took place. Californians continued celebrating for two more days, when they learned by telegraph that the ceremony would take place on May 10.

The Last Spike Ceremony

Newspapers had assigned their star reporters to describe the historic joining of Central Pacific and Union Pacific tracks. Tourists, anxious to attend "the marriage of the rails" ceremony, also gathered at the desolate desert site of Promontory Summit.[4]

It wasn't raining on Monday, May 10, but it was cloudy and cold. During the early morning, shivering spectators watched construction workers complete all but the final connecting rail. Shortly before 9 a.m. Stanford rolled up in his train. He had to wait an hour before Durant alighted from his luxurious train car. Another Union Pacific train brought four companies of infantrymen and a delegation of Mormons, both with their own band. Soldiers were stationed along the tracks to hold back crowds that were pushing and shoving for front-line places. Bands played and locomotives whistled while an unruly, impatient audience waited.

At noon General Dodge stepped forward and lifted his hand for silence. Ceremonies started. Workers brought a laurel-wood tie from Stanford's coach, placed it down, then laid the last rail sections across it. Special spikes were handed to Stanford and Durant: two made of California gold, one of Nevada silver, and another, from Arizona, consisting of iron, silver, and gold. The men dropped them into holes that had been drilled in advance into the laurel-wood tie.

People, including reporters, did not know that the precious metal spikes and tie were quickly removed and replaced by ordinary iron spikes, and a pine tie. One of the spikes and an iron hammer were both wired to the Transcontinental Telegraph line so that the nation could "hear" the final blows that would link Union Pacific and Central Pacific lines.

The ritual was boring. Two ministers offered prayers. Stanford and Dodge gave speeches. Mr. Shilling, the telegraph operator whose table was stationed close to the

A lofty view

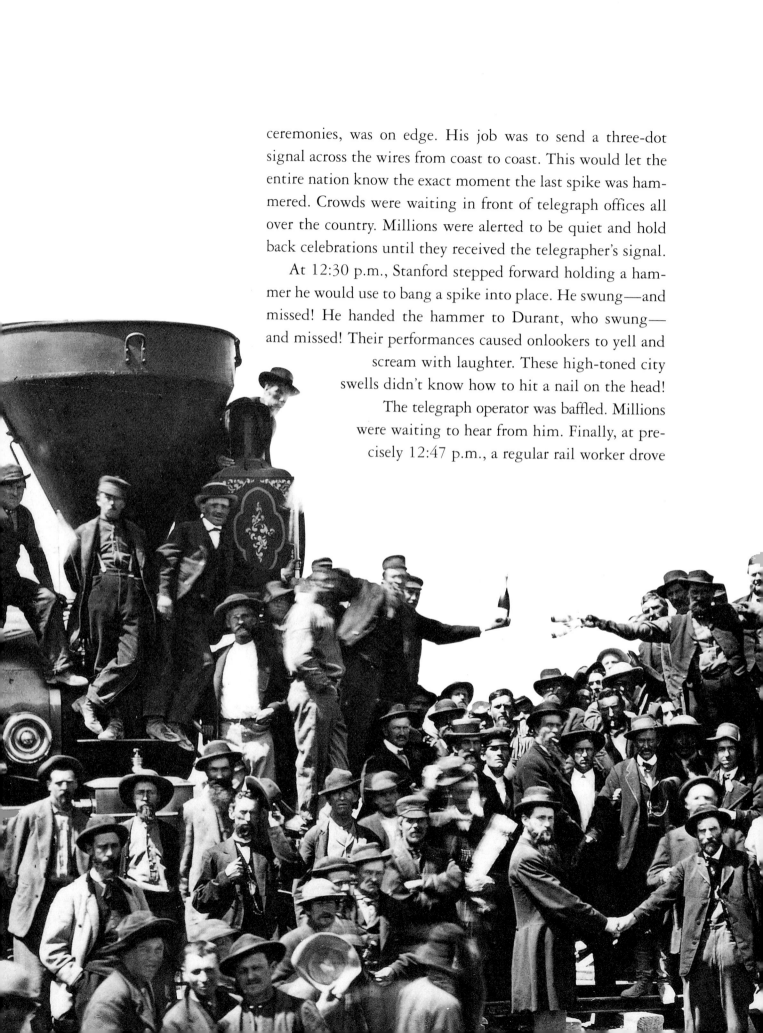

ceremonies, was on edge. His job was to send a three-dot signal across the wires from coast to coast. This would let the entire nation know the exact moment the last spike was hammered. Crowds were waiting in front of telegraph offices all over the country. Millions were alerted to be quiet and hold back celebrations until they received the telegrapher's signal.

At 12:30 p.m., Stanford stepped forward holding a hammer he would use to bang a spike into place. He swung—and missed! He handed the hammer to Durant, who swung—and missed! Their performances caused onlookers to yell and scream with laughter. These high-toned city swells didn't know how to hit a nail on the head!

The telegraph operator was baffled. Millions were waiting to hear from him. Finally, at precisely 12:47 p.m., a regular rail worker drove home the last spike, and Mr. Shilling of Western Union tapped three dots, signifying "done."

When the Central Pacific's handsome locomotive, *Jupiter*, and the Union Pacific's more ordinary Engine Number 119 faced each other at the last tie, the engineers shook hands, and smashed bottles of champagne against each other's locomotives. The rival crews cheered each other. Durant shook hands with Stanford and cried out, "There is henceforth but one Pacific Railroad in the United States."[5]

There was pandemonium.

Souvenir hunters attacked. They hunted in vain for gold and silver spikes, then used jackknives to

Celebrating the union of two railroads

Railroads built by **1850**

Railroads built by **1870**

Railroads built by **1890**

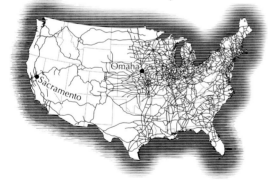

whittle away ties and chip flakes from iron rails. Liquor flowed over locomotives, onto the tracks, and down peoples' throats. A beef salesmen who was part of the crowd recalled, "It was a very hilarious occasion; everybody had all they wanted to drink all the time.... I do not remember what any of the speakers said, but I do remember that there was a great abundance of champagne."[6]

This historic event was neither dignified nor inspirational. Everybody yelled "fit to bust."[7] There was so much pushing and shoving that newspaper reporters couldn't get up front to see or hear what was going on. Their articles contained details that were told to them, that they assumed took place, or that they made up. Descriptions of a golden spike being the last spike made a good story, even though this was not so.[8]

The three-dot code meaning "done" triggered celebrations all over the country. People went wild with excitement. Factory whistles sounded, bells pealed, fireworks crackled, and crowds converged to party in the streets. The old Liberty Bell was struck in Philadelphia. A parade seven miles long was staged in Chicago. A ball on a pole that had been specially set above Washington's Capitol dome dropped while watching crowds roared. A 200-gun salute took place in New York City, and a 100-cannon salvo thundered in Omaha. Banquets and parties lasted throughout the night.

Dodge recalled that, after the ceremony at Promontory Summit, officials and important guests "took refuge in the Central Pacific cars where wine flowed freely," and telegrams

Rail travel for the rich could be luxurious.

were sent and received.[9] A wire dispatched to President Ulysses S. Grant read: "The last rail is laid. The last spike is driven. The Pacific Railroad is completed. The point of junction is 1,086 miles west of the Missouri River, and 690 miles east of Sacramento City. [signed] Leland Stanford, Central Pacific Railroad; T.C. Durant, Union Pacific Railroad."[10]

No date in United States history could have been more exciting or full of promise. National celebrations of the Last Spike Ceremony marked an event that was as significant for Americans in 1869 as the first landing on the moon was a hundred years later. Six years after the ground-breaking ceremony in Sacramento, space had been conquered. Iron rails finally spanned the continent; two oceans had been linked. Because of the new Pacific Railroad—a combination of the Union Pacific and the Central Pacific Companies—travel and trade between the Atlantic and Pacific coasts could be accomplished with incredible speed.

Crossing the continent by train took only a week!

The Union Pacific and Central Pacific had opened up a new West. Their race became part of the American legend, and it set the stage for a new era of expansion. Railroad workers had proved that neither mountains, nor snows, nor deserts could keep the country from going forward, full steam ahead.

FOLLOWING PAGES: Indians, frontiersmen, pioneer families, and investors headed West by train from the Union Pacific depot in Omaha, Nebraska.

NOTES

PART 1 Getting Started

Introduction

1. Dee Brown, *Hear That Lonesome Whistle Blow*, p. 28.

2. December 30, 1853, James Gadsden of South Carolina was authorized to buy 45,535 square miles of northern Mexico from the Mexican government. The Gadsden Purchase cost ten million dollars.

3. Robert Howard, *The Great Iron Trail*, p. 91.

1 "Crazy Judah"

1. It would run from Dutch Flat Mining Camp through Donner Pass and the Truckee River canyon, then down to the Washoe silver-rich country of Nevada.

2. The pamphlet was published in 1857.

3. John Williams, *A Great and Shining Road*, pp. 6, 34.

4. George Kraus, *High Road to Promontory*, p. 30.

5. *Ibid.*, p. 31.

6. Although the Far West was a comfortable distance from Civil War battle fronts, people were concerned about the outcome of the war. Political leaders in California were

pro-Union; only a small segment of Southerners who had settled on the West Coast wanted California to back the Confederacy.

7. Kraus, p. 35.

8. Dee Brown, *Hear That Lonesome Whistle Blow,* p. 48.

9. *Ibid.,* p. 49.

10. Kraus, p. 51.

11. *Ibid.,* p. 50.

12. John Williams, *A Great and Shining Road,* p. 49.

13. Kraus, p. 58.

14. *Ibid.,* p. 59. The Sacramento *Union* quoted.

15. In 1867 the Big Four formed the Contract and Finance Company in place of the Crocker Contracting Company.

2 Stalled Near Mountains

1. Garry Hogg, *Union Pacific,* p. 3.

2. *Ibid.,* p. 39.

3. George Kraus, *High Road to Promontory,* p. 100.

4. James McCague, *Moguls and Iron Men,* p. 225. San Francisco's *Alta California* newspaper quoted.

3 "Not a Chinaman's Chance"

1. Richard O'Connor, *Iron Wheels and Broken Men,* p. 74.

2. Stan Steiner, *Fusang: The Chinese Who Built America,* p. 131.

3. Ibid., p. 132.

4. Ibid., p. 130.

5. Ibid., p. 130.

6. George Kraus, *High Road to Promontory*, p. 111.

There were no accurate records kept regarding the numbers of Chinese who worked for the Central Pacific. Estimates vary between 5,000 and 15,000.

7. Steiner, p. 30.

8. Lynne Mayer & Kenneth Vose, *Makin' Tracks*, p. 31.

9. John Williams, *The Great and Shining Road*, p. 161.

10. Simon Winchester, *Pacific Rising*, p. 234. The newspaper report appeared in 1870, one year after the railroad had been completed.

4 Tracks Across the Desert

1. Lynne Mayer & Kenneth Vose, *Makin' Tracks*, p. 61.

2. John Williams, *A Great and Shining Road*, p. 211.

3. *Ibid.*, p. 206.

4. Mr. Lake's willingness to part with his land was self-serving. Increased traffic meant more money for him because he collected tolls from everyone who walked or rode across a bridge that he refused to sell.

5. George Kraus, *High Road to Promontory*, p. 198.

6. Charlton Ogburn, *Railroads*, p. 61. Strobridge's notes quoted.

7. William Rae, *Westward by Rail*, p. 217.

8. Dee Brown, *Hear That Lonesome Whistle Blow*, p. 101.

9. The engineer, J. M. Graham, never explained how this story was "told" by Indians to Chinese. See Kraus, p. 201.

10. Strobridge refused to acknowledge the danger because he failed to find the skeletons of dead travelers along the way. See James McGague, *Moguls and Iron Men*, p. 373.

11. Wesley Griswold, *A Work of Giants*, p. 246.

12. Quoted from a detailed report by W. H. Rhodes, correspondent for the *San Francisco Chronicle*. See Kraus, p. 210.

PART 2   Heading West

5 The Rival Railroad

1. Grenville Dodge, *How We Built the Union Pacific*, p. 10.

2. Charles Ames, *Pioneering the Union Pacific*, p. 12.

3. Willis Thornton, *The Nine Lives of Citizen Train*, p. 145.

In 1870 Train became the inspiration for Jules Verne's book after Train went around the world in 80 days. Train ran for President of the United States in 1872.

4. John Williams, *A Great and Shining Road*, p. 53. Train quoted.

5. Richard Ketchum, "Faces from the Past," *American Heritage*, April 1963, p. 39.

6. Williams, p. 84.

7. Wesley Griswold, *A Work of Giants*, p. 15.

8. *Ibid.*, p. 138.

9. Henry Sturgis, "The Iron Spine," *American Heritage*, April 1969, p. 108.

6   An Army on Wheels

1. John Williams, *A Great and Shining Road*, p. 123.

2. Grenville Dodge, *How We Built the Union Pacific*, p. 14.

3. *Ibid.*, p. 31.

4. *Ibid.*, p. 81.

President Lincoln never enjoyed using the luxurious railroad car, which had been built especially for him.

5. Silas Seymour, *Incidents of a Trip Through the Great Platte Valley to the Rocky Mountains and Laramie Plains in the Fall of 1866*, pp. 41, 85.

6. *Ibid.*, p. 87.

7. *Ibid.*, p. 89.

8. *Ibid.*, p. 90.

9. *Ibid.*, p. 100.

10. *Ibid.*, p. 103.

11. *Ibid.*, p. 109.

7 "Wild Indians"

1. Samuel Bowles, *Our New West*, pp. 155-57. Bowles was the editor of the Springfield, Massachusetts, newspaper, *Republic*.

2. When the treaty came before the Senate, terms were reduced to ten years, with the possibility of extension for another five.

3. Ralph Andrist, *The Long Death*, p. 89.

4. Prisoners who were set free for frontier service were known as "galvanized Yankees," and "white-washed Rebels." Officially they were called "U. S. Volunteers."

5. President Johnson's Secretary of Interior, Orville Browning, was vehemently opposed to sponsoring the Union Pacific. He also expressed deep-seated dislike for Generals Grant, Sherman, and Dodge. He opposed the Army's Indian policy.

6. J. R. Perkins, *Trails, Rails, and War*, p. 181.

7. Andrist, p. 108.

8. *Ibid.*, p. 124.

9. Wesley Griswold, *A Work of Giants*, p. 216.

10. *Ibid.*, p. 216.

11. B. A. Botkin and Alvin Harlow, *A Treasury of Railroad Folklore*, p. 118.

'12. The sixth, William Thompson, was scalped, yet survived by "playing dead." In the dark of night, he sneaked off carrying his own scalp which had slipped off his attacker's belt. Thompson staggered four miles to a railroad station at Plum Creek. Eventually he took a train to Omaha, hoping that a surgeon could sew his scalp onto his head. The operation failed, but Thompson's fame lives on. His scalp became a popular attraction in the Boys-and-Girls' Room of the Omaha Public Library where it was exhibited until 1985. It is now in the Union Pacific Museum in Omaha.

13. The conductor and three other men ran down the tracks and stopped another freight train, which then backed up to the nearest station, at Plum Creek.

14. Buffalo Bill Cody, the most famous hunter, boasted that he had killed 4,280 buffalo in 18 months. He worked for the Union Pacific Southern Division (the Kansas Pacific) until 1868. Beginning in the 1880s, he staged lavish Wild West shows that were immensely popular and toured in Europe and the United States until 1913. The content of these shows, which included Indian raids and buffalo hunts, was not unlike some of the entertainments staged by the Union Pacific Railroad.

15. Lynne Mayer & Kenneth Vose, *Makin' Tracks*, p. 98.

8 Gaining Ground

1. Samuel Bowles, *Our New West*, p. 56.

2. Robert Athearn, *Union Pacific Country*, p. 61.

North Platte is a major Union Pacific town today with hundreds of employees and a vast railyard.

3. John Williams, *A Great and Shining Road*, p. 155.

4. *Ibid.*, p. 157.

5. Wesley Griswold, *A Work of Giants*, p. 225.

6. James McCague, *Moguls and Iron Men*, p. 237.

7. *Ibid.*, p. 52.

8. Samuel Bowles, *Our New West*, p. 56.

9. George Kraus, *High Road to Promontory*, p. 203. San Francisco's *Alta California* newspaper quoted.

10. Lynne Mayer & Kenneth Vose, *Makin' Tracks*, p. 125.

11. Athearn, p. 148. Quoted from an 1867 journal.

12. McCague, pp. 189, 190.

13. The Homestead Act seemed to be a blessing, but it had flaws that caused many people much suffering. Farms far from the railroad were of little value because crops couldn't be shipped out to major markets. And although 160 acres were ideally suited to farmers in the fertile lands of the East, those who settled on the Great Plains needed at least four times that amount to survive the droughts, cloudbursts, dust storms, and

blizzards. During the 1860s, homesteaders entrenched no farther than 300 miles past Omaha fared quite well.

9 The Great Race

1. Grenville Dodge, *How We Built the Union Pacific Railway*, p. 23.

2. The Utah Central Railroad was completed in January 1870.

3. Dodge, p. 24.

4. *Ibid,* p. 24.

5. Robert Athearn, *Union Pacific Country*, pp. 114-15.

6. Charles Ames, *Pioneering the Union Pacific*, p. 318.

10 A Grand Celebration

1. According to a popular story, Durant had bet Crocker $10,000 that ten miles in a day couldn't be done. However, there is no reliable record that the bet was ever made or paid.

2. Wesley Griswold, *A Work of Giants*, p. 317.

3. *New York Times*, May 11, 1869.

4. Many books, magazines, and television productions mistakenly name Promontory Point as the place famous for the Golden Spike Ceremony. The historic event took place at Promontory Summit, which is 24 miles away.

5. *New York Times*, May 11, 1869.

6. B. A. Botkin and Alvin Harlow, *A Treasury of Railroad Folklore*, p. 124.

7. James McCague, *Moguls and Iron Men*, p. 331.

8. According to many erroneous accounts, both Stanford and Durant used a silver hammer and missed hitting a golden spike.

9. Grenville Dodge, *How We Built the Union Pacific Railway*, p. 25.

10. *New York Times*, May 11, 1869.

"A Good Square American Smile"
The Union Pacific deserves only part of the smile—
from Omaha, Nebraska, to Promontory Summit, Utah.
The Central Pacific finished the "grin" to the Pacific, and
other railroads extended the country's happy face
to the Atlantic Ocean.

BIBLIOGRAPHY

PRIMARY SOURCES

Bowles, Samuel. *Our New West.* Hartford, Conn.: Hartford Publishing Co., 1869.

——. *Across the Continent.* Springfield, Mass.: S. Bowles & Co, 1866.

——. *The Pacific Railroad Open; How to Go; What to See.* Boston, Mass.: Fields, Osgood & Co., 1869.

Dodge, Grenville. *How We Built the Union Pacific Railway.* Washington, D.C., 1910.

Rae, W. F. *Westward By Rail: The New Route to the Far East.* New York, 1871. Reprinted New York, Promontory Press, 1974.

Seymour, Silas. *Incidents of a Trip Through the Great Platte Valley to the Rocky Mountains and Laramie Plains in the Fall of 1866.* New York, 1867.

Train, George. *My Life in Many States and in Foreign Lands.* New York: D. Appleton, 1902.

Union Pacific Railroad Company. *The Great Union Pacific Railroad Excursion to the Hundredth Meridian.* Chicago, 1867.

NEWSPAPERS

Harper's Weekly (1862 through 1870)

New York Times (1862 through 1870)

SECONDARY SOURCES

Ames, Charles. *Pioneering the Union Pacific.* New York: Appleton-Century-Crofts, 1969.

Andrist, Ralph. *The Long Death.* New York: Macmillan Publishing Co., 1964.

Athearn, Robert. *Union Pacific Country.* Lincoln and London: University of Nebraska Press, 1971.

Beebe, Lucius. *The Central Pacific and the Southern Pacific Railroads.* Berkeley, California: Howell-North Press, 1963.

Best, Gerald. *Iron Horses to Promontory.* San Marino, California: Golden West Books, 1969.

Billington, Ray. *The Westward Movement in the United States.* Princeton, New Jersey: D. Van Nostrand Co., Inc., 1959.

Botkin, B. A. and Harlow, Alvin. *A Treasury of Railroad Folklore.* New York: Crown Publishers, 1953.

Brown, Dee. *Hear That Lonesome Whistle Blow.* New York: Holt, Rinehart & Winston, 1977.

Dary, David. *The Buffalo Book.* New York: Avon Books, 1973.

Dick, Everett. *The Lure of the Land.* Lincoln, Nebraska: University of Nebraska Press, 1970.

Frazier, Ian. *Great Plains.* New York: Farrar, Straus & Giroux, 1989.

Galloway, John. *The First Transcontinental Railroad.* New York: Dorset Press, 1990.

Griswold, Wesley. *A Work of Giants.* New York: McGraw Hill, 1962.

Holbrook, Stewart. *The Story of American Railroads.* New York: Crown Publishers, 1947.

Howard, Robert. *The Great Iron Trail.* New York: G. P. Putnam's Sons, 1962.

Hogg, Garry. *Union Pacific.* New York: Walker and Co., 1967.

Huneke, William. *The Government and the Union Pacific.* New York: Garland Publishing, Inc., 1985.

Jensen, Oliver. *The American Heritage History of the Railroad in America.* New York: American Heritage Publishing Co., 1975.

Klein, Maury. *Union Pacific.* New York: Walker and Co., 1987.

Ketchum, Richard. "Faces of the Past." *American Heritage,* April 1963.

Kraus, George. *High Road to Promontory.* Palo Alto, California: Castle Books, 1969.

Lewis, Oscar. *The Big Four.* New York: Alfred A. Knopf, 1938.

Mayer, Lynne, & Vose, Kenneth. *Makin' Tracks.* New York: Praeger Publishers, 1975.

McCague, James. *Moguls and Iron Men.* New York: Harper & Row, 1964.

Ogburn, Charlton. *Railroads: The Great American Adventure.* Washington, D.C.: National Geographic Society, 1973.

O'Connor, Richard. *Iron Wheels and Broken Men.* New York: G. P. Putnam's Sons, 1977.

Paul, Rodman. *The Far West and the Great Plains in Transition.* New York: Harper & Row, 1988.

Perkins, Jacob. *Trails, Rails, and War: The Life of General G. M. Dodge.* Indianapolis: The Bobbs-Merrill Co., 1929.

Steiner, Stan. *Fusang: The Chinese Who Built America.* New York: Harper Colophon Books, 1979.

Sturgis, Henry. "The Iron Spine," *American Heritage,* April 1969.

Thorton, Willis. *The Nine Lives of Citizen Train*, New York: Greenberg, 1948.

Utley, Robert. *The Indian Frontier of the American West 1846-1890.* Albuquerque, New Mexico: University of New Mexico Press, 1984.

Utley, Robert and Washburn, Wilcomb. *Indian Wars.* New York: Houghton Mifflin, 1985.

White, Richard. *A New History of the American West.* Norman, Oklahoma: University of Oklahoma Press, 1991.

Williams, John. *A Great and Shining Road.* New York: Times Books, 1988.

Winchester, Simon. *Pacific Rising.* New York: Prentice Hall Press, 1991.

ILLUSTRATIONS CREDITS

In addition to illustrations from newspapers, periodicals, and books of the 1860s, we are fortunate to view the work of "official photographers" hired by both the Central Pacific Railroad Company and the Union Pacific Railroad Company.

These photographers followed the tracks. By lugging along their heavy, cumbersome equipment and setting up in rough territory, they produced pictures of historic importance. They documented the building of America's first transcontinental railroad. Andrew J. Russell, hired by the Union Pacific, gained fame as a result of his dramatic pictures that show such scenes as men laying tracks (p. 80), building a railroad bridge (pp. 120-121), and celebrating the union of the two railroads (pp. 138-139).

Rhoda Blumberg used the following sources to obtain period illustrations and photographs:

Cover, pp. 2, 15, The Harry T. Peters Collection, Museum of the City of New York; pp. 10-11, Wells Fargo Bank, San Francisco; p. 12, The Granger Collection, New York; pp. 16-17, 18, 73, 74-75, 89 (upper), 120-121,138-139, Courtesy of the Oakland Museum of California; pp. 19, 56-57, 129, 130-131, Southern Pacific Railroad; pp. 5, 22-23, 28-29, 42, 94, 96, 102-103, 109, 118, 127, 142-143, 151, Reproduced from the Collections of the Library of Congress; pp. 38, 41, 46-47, Courtesy, The Bancroft Library; p. 43, Haynes Foundation Collection, Montana Historical Society; p. 44, Kem Lee Studio, courtesy of Kan's Restaurant, San Francisco; p. 52, 132-133, 137, California State Library; pp. 55, 67, 141, New York Public Library; pp. 62-63, From Samuel Bowles, *Our New West*, 1869; p. 64, University of Iowa Libraries; pp. 70-71, 75 (upper), 78-79, 80, 110-111, 135, 136, Union Pacific Museum Collection; pp. 77, 89 (lower), 93, 124-125, National Archives; pp. 83, 84-85, Collection of the New York Historical Society; p. 90, Courtesy, Dept. of Library Services, American Museum of Natural History; p. 92, Colorado Historical Society; p. 99, The Kansas State Historical Society, Topeka, Kansas; p. 104, Walters Art Gallery; p. 105, Western History Dept., Denver Public Library; p. 108, The Nevada Historical Society; p. 114, State Historical Society of Wisconsin; pp. 115, 117, Nebraska State Historical Society; p. 116, The Newberry Library, Chicago; p. 123, Church of Jesus Christ Latter-Day Saints, Salt Lake City.

INDEX

Illustrations are indicated by **boldface**. If illustrations are included within a page span, the entire span is boldface. Material in the Notes has been indexed, with the page and note number (n) given.

RHODA BLUMBERG has been acclaimed for her masterful presentations of landmark events in American history. *School Library Journal* commented that the author "shines in the imaginative use of extensive research to tell, compellingly and entertainingly, stories from history."

Rhoda Blumberg writes about the opening of Japan (1853-1854) in *Commodore Perry in the Land of the Shogun*, a 1986 Newbery Honor Book, which also won the Boston Globe/Horn Book Award and the Golden Kite Award. *The Incredible Journey of Lewis and Clark*, about the famed expedition (1804-1806) is a Golden Kite Award winner, and *The Great American Gold Rush* (which chiefly took place between 1848-1852) won the John and Patricia Beatty Award, given by the California Library Association. Each of these titles and *The Remarkable Voyages of Captain Cook* have been chosen as ALA Notable Books.

Rhoda Blumberg and her husband, Gerald, live in Yorktown Heights, New York.

THE WORLD'S LARGEST NONPROFIT SCIENTIFIC AND EDUCATIONAL ORGANIZATION, THE NATIONAL GEOGRAPHIC SOCIETY WAS FOUNDED IN 1888 "FOR THE INCREASE AND DIFFUSION OF GEOGRAPHIC KNOWLEDGE." FULFILLING THIS MISSION, THE SOCIETY EDUCATES AND INSPIRES MILLIONS EVERYDAY THROUGH MAGAZINES, BOOKS, TELEVISION PROGRAMS, VIDEOS, MAPS AND ATLASES, RESEARCH GRANTS, THE NATIONAL GEOGRAPHY BEE, TEACHER WORKSHOPS, AND INNOVATIVE CLASSROOM MATERIALS. THE SOCIETY IS SUPPORTED THROUGH MEMBERSHIP DUES AND INCOME FROM THE SALE OF ITS EDUCATIONAL PRODUCTS. CALL 1-800-NGS-LINE FOR MORE INFORMATION.